AF411526

TABLE OF CONTENTS

A blue orb in a black abyss. This image of our planet from space is now commonplace. It is in my lifetime, however, that it was first captured and shared with the world. In the fifty or so years since, increasing evidence affirms the significance of such a comprehensive view. Seen as a whole, we can no longer distinguish "Nature" as a place apart or separate from human endeavor and inhabitation. We are immersed in and shaped by it. Embracing this simultaneity of our earthly existence—a balanced interchange of natural forces and the art and labor of human settlement—is essential to how we live and design.

"Structuring Confluence" records our struggle to shape human experience around this relationship and to make it palpable and engaging. As cities become the dominant habitat for our species, we are working to forge new forms and places that responsibly and artfully synthesize ecology and urbanism. Organized by place, our research into forces working on a site at many scales leads us sometimes into remote areas of inquiry. Embedding isolated processes into new networks creates unexpected bonds and opportunities which can provide new meaning. This book provides a glimpse of the results of that invention process. It is composed of a personal selection of projects from my 13 years of practice in NYC connected by a series of structuring ideas. It simultaneously is an homage to the many people who have contributed their talents to its development—colleagues, studio members, consultants, and of course clients, whose foresight and courage can greatly influence the course of a project.

Water and its fluid dynamics have always fascinated and inspired me. Though most cities are shaped by and around their relationships to bodies of water, the aqueous element remains largely unrepresented in urban life. Often rerouted or piped underground, the invisible hydrological network prevents us from understanding the critical role water plays in the ecosystem of which we are a part. It also denies us the delight of engaging with its ceaseless transience and refreshing vibrancy. Our work in NYC began with the impulse to privilege the forces of water and has evolved to acknowledge a more complex confluence of social and ecological relationships. By structuring history, landforms and movement, uses and experience, and forests and other vegetation, we hope to imbue a place with vitality and meaning. Celebrating what makes a place unique by uncovering these dormant relationships and finding new ways to make them manifest is what inspires us.

In this last year, while writing this book, Superstorm Sandy in NYC, floods in Europe, and most recently floods in Calgary and Denver, have forcefully demonstrated humans' impact on water systems and cycles. The necessity for action can no longer be ignored. As the "why" becomes more clear, the "how" becomes more critical. Design can help build consensus towards new ways of living in nature, with places and experiences that engage and stimulate us. Structuring Confluence presents a process that unites science and art to forge new territories of engagement and discovery, and creates more sustainable relationships between ourselves, our communities and the earth.

BARBARA WILKS

Eric W. Sanderson

THE TOTAL NATURE OF CITIES

It is in vogue now to talk about the nature in cities. A forest of books and a legion of worthy architectural designs ache to restore a sense of the natural to human-dedicated and dominated places in town. Many of these efforts focus on those patches of semi-natural habitat, the green bits, which are found in all cities, and which can be encouraged or discouraged by human action. God bless them all. Some of the designs you will find in this book are of the same kind, but others have taken on a larger idea of how cities fit into nature. But what I want to write about is something different: the total nature of cities.

I want us to conceive of cities in their entirety as ecological places, or more precisely, as ecological landscapes. To an ecologist like me, the landscape is the pattern and process of the ecosystems found in a place. In a wilder place, we might talk of the landscape as composed of a conifer forest with a sinuous stream beside a mountain cliff. The patterns are not just the ways the stream curves along the forested edge, but how the stream and the forest make habitat for tanagers, trout, and bears. The processes are the interactions of the bears with the trout (food on the one hand, fear on the other), and the way the marshy bit near the cliff where the tanager lingers also absorbs the flood cascading down the mountain.

In the city, the buildings, streets, boardwalks, sidewalks and parking lots, ball fields, basketball courts, fountains, and power plants, as well as the green bits, are the landscape. Like in a "natural" landscape, an "urban" landscape is a complex and evolving mosaic, where natural things happen. Perhaps it is no longer a place for bears or trout, but other creatures inhabit it, and long for the resilience that comes from flood-stopping and beauty of streams flowing.

Michael Sorkin

NATURE AND NOT

It's always been tough to tell nature and culture apart. The pervasive idea of a creator, a celestial designer, a cosmic Capability Brown, continues to infuse the way we situate ourselves within the web of life. Whether in the absurdities of arguments from "intelligent design" or the more rigorous prescriptions of evolution, the styles in which we comprehend the motives behind the forms of our environment define the character of our own autonomy.

This grappling with questions of whether we're in or out of nature is imbued with the myth of paradise, with our expulsion from that lovely garden of total irresponsibility. Such fantasies gave rise to competing theories of whether we've fallen from an ideal state of continuity with the natural—predicated on our pre-lapsarian ignorance before we bit into that forbidden Granny Smith—or whether we've risen above it to lord it over all the other creatures great and small. The great 18th century debates about states of nature – whether they represented a condition of total harmoniousness or a brutal war of all against all—form part of the bedrock not simply of moral philosophy but of way in which we understand the "landscape."

By nature (and natural) I mean the interactions of soil and rock, air and water, energy and life, that characterize our verdant planet, and by natural, I mean the qualities of everyone and everything that participates in the great congress of life on Earth, including you and me. Those interactions and those qualities do not disappear when we build a city. Rather, they take on new, idiosyncratic forms, which contrast in many ordinary and extraordinary ways with the ecological mosaics that formerly filled the place where the city now stands.

For example, consider the fascinating work from Nova Scotia, where Jeremy Lundholm and Ashley Marlin[1] surveyed the plants living in the cracks of sidewalks, the edges of the lawns, and other corners of the city of Halifax, and then traced back those plants, which most of us would think only as weeds, to the ecological niches where they were originally found in the world. They found that Halifax city plants have affinities with species that normally inhabit cliffs and talus slopes, and less commonly, grasslands and floodplains. Sidewalks are, from these plants' perspective, a cliff on its side.

[1] Lundholm, J.T. and A. Marlin. 2006. Habitat origins and microhabitat preferences of urban plant species. Urban Ecosystems 9:139-159

Lundholm's open-minded inquiries are on to something: can we read an urban landscape "naturally"? Perhaps with analogues we can. Let's let tall buildings stand in for cliffy hills, notice how gutters guide bubbling streams during a storm, observe sidewalks as animal trails with regular patterns of use in morning and evening. Let's talk about the evaporation coming out of grates on a cold Manhattan morning in the same breath as the evapotranspiration from trees on a summer afternoon, for both flows are part of a hydrological cycle returning rain water from the ground to the atmosphere. Let's find out how biological matter passes through an ecosystem, whether that biomass is measured in leaves falling from a tree, or sandwiches passing through the deli door. The nature of cities requires us to broaden our sense of what nature is.

At the same time that these twin philosophical theories of the state of nature were formulated, the practices of landscape architecture also became articulate. In the standard western telling of the tale (of course, Asian landscape traditions were longstanding but only filtered into our consciousness as the result of the colonial enterprise), another double sensibility—identified with the French and the English—arose. According to this history, the French tradition was formal, "rational," and was permeated by geometric forms and radical discipline of plant materials, held in Euclidian bondage. The English style, on the other hand, was artfully composed to give the appearance of romantic "wildness," meant to appear not designed but found.

Of course, there was a parallel development as agriculture and forestry grew in scale and technological sophistication, representing a functionalist other that has always been the predominant form of terrestrial cultivation but which has long been aesthetically invisible, just "part of the landscape". As I write this, I am riding in a car through a heavily afforested area of northern China and am looking at the way in which the deliberate forests all around me are planted in a strict grid rather than according to the more natural (dis)order engendered by wind and birds and shade and "accident." Tomorrow I'll fly home over the American west with its own massive geometries of the mile-square grid and the profusion of irrigated circles, land brought under control—made productive—by its efficiently ordering geometry, conducing the legible transformation of nature into property, much to the chagrin of Native Americans whose metaphysic of property and pattern was altogether different.

This same dialectic of order and disorder—rather of two aesthetics of order—reached a sublime balance with the extension of the Manhattan grid after 1811 and the design and development of Central Park. One might argue that this arrangement—disorder within order—is a conceptual flipping of the English tradition, in which a highly rational, acutely geometric, Georgian manor house was inscribed within a wild landscape, reflected a deft reversal of relations to characterize the difference between the country and the city. This occurred at the moment at which, as Raymond Williams and others have pointed out, the country was itself being urbanized, at which capitalist relations of property—reflected in the English enclosure laws—were being inscribed on feudal patterns and which produced people who were living according to urban habits and rituals in the countryside.

All this grappling with the representation of nature grew from the rise in actual scientific understanding. This included Linnean taxonomy and the impetus—not unrelated to the project of global colonialism—to identify (and collect) every species, every mineral, every culture: to possess them all. The sense of a vast planetary encyclopedia continues to shape our own consciousness, both in terms of the environmentalist anxiety about the disappearance of species due to anthropogenically-induced extinctions, which threaten both our bio-diversity—our absolute faith—and give rise to more specialized fears, ranging from the possibility that the plant that's just gone under forever might have been the cure for cancer to a more free-form dread of a homogenizing sphere in which all cultures and human variety are converging on cyborg forms of multinational control.

Of course part of what we are broadening to include is us. In ancient texts, nature was commonly contrasted with artifice: artifice is what people create; nature is what is created without us. What a terrible notion! Terrible on two counts. Terrible on the first count, because it suggests an equivalency, as if one species (people) were somehow equivalent in creative powers to everything else on Earth, an idea ludicrous and arrogant, no matter how much we may delight privately in our own inventions. Terrible on the second count, because it suggests a sundering, a division of us from our world. Rather than seeing us as participants in the network of life, which we manifestly are, we instead imagine we are removed and separate. Much havoc has been wreaked on the backs of these misconceptions, with not the least of the mayhem originating from cities.

John Muir, the famous naturalist, once wrote: "When we try to pick out anything by itself we find that it is bound fast by a thousand invisible cords that cannot be broken, to everything in the universe." That dictum is a mainstay of the conservation movement, but it is wrong in certain respects (as intuitions often are). Not everything is connected to everything, but in fact there are distinct patterns to the connections. Moreover those connections can certainly be broken. In fact one of the wonders of nature is how it continues to persist all around us despite the many ways in which one species – our species – shatters connections right and left. Cities, in the minds of many in the conservation world, are conceived as the archetype of that destruction. But they too miss the point. People too need a place to live, and if a city can provide art, culture, and a job, who is to say that our need for a corner of God's green earth is less or more important than another species?

The modern acculturation of the landscape was made particularly precise by Darwinism and our subsequent understanding of the genetic basis for the process of evolution, a set of ideas that potentiated another species of dynamism in the way we look at natural systems. The scientific school of ecology that grew around evolutionary theory and its ideas about speciation was quickly transmuted into the urban theory, in particular via the Chicago school and in the work of Patrick Geddes and his successors. These brought the growth and differentiation of cities under the metaphorical regime of ecology and evolution and this "master narrative" continues to inform our thinking about urban behavior, as well as our on-going angst about our own dominion.

Today, we are in the midst of a major re-understanding of the relationship between cities and nature, and the theoretical territory is contested by a number of vaguely differentiated schools of thought, including landscape urbanists, new urbanists, ecological urbanists, ad infinitum. What all have recognized is the need to recalibrate the relationship between cities and the earth in light of exponential urban growth (more than half the planet now lives in cities), the massive deterioration of the environment due to human activities, and the insane levels of inequality that the neo-liberal economy is producing. We are coming to be chillingly aware of the possibility that we will exceed (may already have exceeded) the bearing capacity of the earth: by one estimate, if everyone were to consume at the rate of the US, we would need an additional three planets to supply our needs.

And so the subject of "landscape" is reintroduced into the discussion of cities as a form of corrective re-understanding. For many, this is just window dressing, an ornamental tithe to the parlous fate of the earth. For others, though, it is a gateway to a set of metrics — the algorithms of our ecological footprints — that can undergird a clarity of values in urban design and lead to a far more nuanced understanding of the behavior of both our cities and ourselves in planetary terms. The calculus of necessary food, water, oxygen, energy, manufacturing, bio-diversity, etc. has finally become explicitly foundational in the way we do our work. The recent wake-up calls received from the news that global CO_2 has passed 400 parts per million for the first time in several million years, from the shocks of highly destructive and energetic storms like Sandy, from the melting of the ice caps, and from the sheer, alienating, dreariness of our burgeoning megacities, are directing us to rethink our practices, to argue that they are authentically commensurate with the scale of the problems we confront.

Let us reconceive. What are cities? Cities are, definitively, constructed habitat for people. Most species in nature come to an environment with whatever skills and characteristics their evolutionary history has provided them with and then they try to fit in. How well they do, whether they survive, depends on how well-suited they are to the new conditions. Cliff plants do well in sidewalks because they are pre-adapted to living in tight places. The human trick is instead of adapting to the environment, we change the environment to adapt to us. Too cold in winter? Build a building and close the window. Not enough food? Domesticate plants and animals and grow a garden. Water levels uncertain? Construct a dam and an aqueduct. Missing nature? How about a park?

How are we able to do these things? It is not through magic or tremendous strength, but because our evolutionary gifts are large and flexible minds, an admirable ability to communicate in language, expression, and deed, and an affinity for each other: we are social like few animals have ever been. Because of these gifts, I can conceive of yesterday and contrast it with today; I can imagine different futures; and I can communicate my ideas with you, through this essay. If you find those ideas have merit, then we can work together to change the environment to match our conception of it. We can even, if we try, change our conceptions to match the environment.

And so we get to the nub of it: the nature of cities. Cities are ecological places, but have rarely been conceived in those terms, despite a history nearly 10,000 years in the making. We can conceive of them however as if their nature mattered. We can recognize the water that falls from the sky. We can acknowledge the soil on which we construct our buildings. We can celebrate the plants and animals that share the city space with us; spaces that we can create by being creative, communicative, flexible, generous. As you turn the pages of this volume, what you will find are examples for inspiration.

Perhaps this will be our 21st century contribution to the notion of urban life, what is not only vogue now, but for all time: that cities are not only places of art, culture, communication, finance, business, science, religion, politics, and economy, but cities are also places for and from and of nature, cities of nature, nature with us definitively in it.

Crucial to designers is, of course, the question of the artistic content of our endeavors. Modernist architectural writ took it as an item of faith that there could be a merger between the social, the technical, and the artistic that offered an almost automated aesthetic. Functionalism suggested that form was the outcome of a series of calculations that would inevitably produce beautiful results: it conceived beauty performatively in the same way an aeronautical engineer or naval architect would find an object elegant to exactly the degree it was economic and efficient. Although this sort of arithmetic can easily turn dark, I don't think it's misplaced to suggest that we need a return to evidence-based forms of architectural, urban, and landscape design, that the effects of our work are a satisfying material basis for constructing an inevitable — but not complete — theory of form.

But a practice becomes art because of some expressive supplement it brings to the table. Functionalism, *inter alia*, was artistic (including the claims to the contrary that formed part of its operation) because it was in energetic dialogue with the forms of expression it sought to supplant (a battle of the styles like every other) and because it embodied a set of formal predilections that were, in fact, completely susceptible to traditional modes of aesthetic analysis. Modernist urbanism foundered, however, on the rigidity — indeed, the stupidity — with which it linked its socially-glossed forms with a vision of urban life that was fundamentally appalling. Not as a critique of the 19th century industrial city — which was an unsustainable and degrading horror — but in the one-dimensionality of its own ideas about replacement.

Today, this battle is rejoined as different formal ideas jostle for the crown of the one true urban or landscape practice. This is an enervating, useless, and distracting struggle, particularly when seen in the environmental context which must more and more be engaged in helping to find the sources of local particularity as they are increasingly winnowed by global stereotypes and moronic simulacra. But, looking in on the landscape profession from my slightly oblique view, I find it both socially and artistically heartening to see the thickening range of forms and practices and the increased attunement to the rhythms and respirations of the city that have come to characterize the work of many. Indeed, it is exactly the capacity of landscape architecture to structure confluence among the disciplines that establishes its special relevance today. Although my own tooth for irony and minimalism is not what it once was, I don't suggest that we abandon either the drollery, abstract heroism, or critical edge they embody: I like gilt bagels and running fences as much as the next aesthete. But there is something so bracing about forms that produce, that shade, that greet the earth with tenderness and redress, that spread the complexity necessary for the widest possible and happiest co-habitation of our only planet.

The projects in this volume do precisely that. To paraphrase: we invent our nature and then it invents us. And then we invent it again.

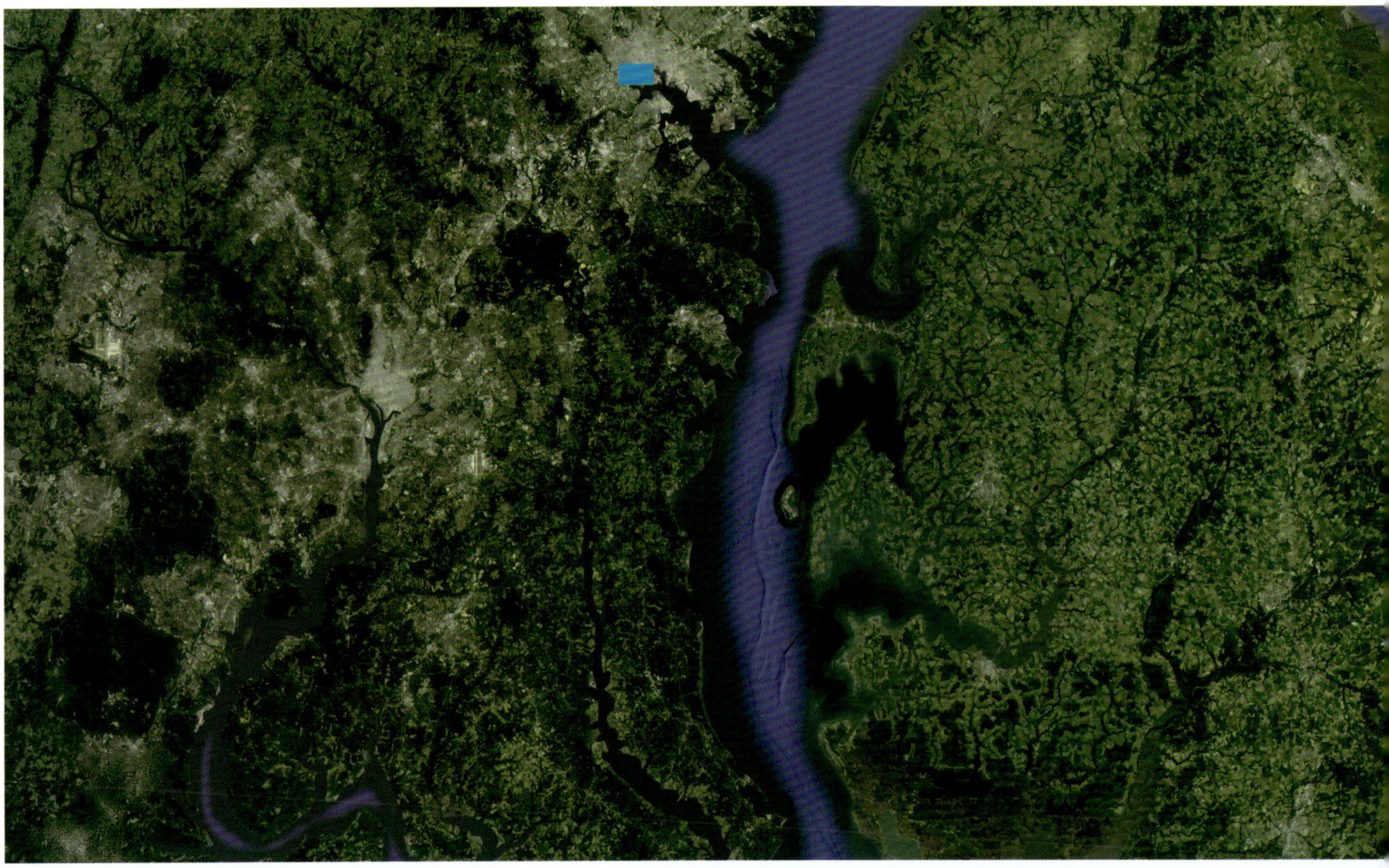

TIDEWATER — BALTIMORE

"Seeing is forgetting the name of the thing one sees."

Robert Irwin as quoted by Lawrence Weschler

1   The Chesapeake Bay
estuary—partial view

2   Baltimore Harbor on the
Patapsco River, a part of the
Chesapeake Bay Estuary

Cities are embedded in nature, but we are often blind to these connections. Looking at a site at different scales often helps us see the various systems of which they are a part, both cultural and ecological. The Chesapeake Bay is one of the largest estuaries in the world, home to vital ecosystems which support a wide range of plant and animal life. Baltimore, Maryland was one of the largest ports in the country, but that and the industries around the harbor are dying, and are in the process of being replaced by recreational and other uses. Projects are sited in both of these systems (and others) simultaneously. Bringing them together in our projects by finding reciprocal relationships is our goal.

TIDE POINT

This fourteen acre site in South Baltimore had been one of Proctor and Gamble's main soap producing plants, once part of a string of industrial pursuits that lined the waterfront beyond the narrow residential streets of Locust Point. There was no going back to Baltimore's industrial and shipping heyday— the future of Tide Point would embrace its past as it looked to the future. Our role here encompassed master planning, landscape architecture, and designing new construction for campus amenities.

Tide Point is an example of how a site can be both preserved and completely transformed. While choosing to keep the site strongly connected to its industrial past, we also embedded it in the ecology of the Chesapeake Bay while opening it to the public. The new focus of the site is the water. We found some resonance between the ever shifting tides of the estuary and the indefinite quality of the ground in the industrial landscape, where land has been filled and metal grated walkways float above tanks, bridges haphazardly connect buildings, and pipes flow in many directions. The concrete of industry still dominates the site, but it becomes a dynamic shifting grid that slips over and under other materials. The grid guides pedestrian use moving towards the waterfront. Gaps allow the site to absorb water and nutrients, providing a 30% increase in permeability which contributes to improvement in the quality of the harbor waters and allows space for hardy native gardens to bloom. The site becomes a sedimentation

of elements, floating up and alongside the pier promenade. Using this tidal flow as the backbone of our design work, not only informed the new name for the site, but serves as a reference point to encompass the myriad cultural and natural histories embodied here.

Though few things are physically made at Tide Point these days, an industrial energy still dominates. We identified many features to leave in place and to incorporate into the new landscape, including foundation walls, concrete tank bases, steel cranes, and tanks. These objects don't decorate the landscape, they form it. An industrial "garden" of old tank bases is a unique gathering space, public art project, and lookout onto the water. Old pipes and cranes shape a water garden nestled in tight space between buildings. An old foundation wall encloses parking. Office space tucks underneath an old trestle. In conjunction with the buildings, these features find new meaning and uses in this new context; a context framed by their existence.

Renamed Tide Point, the campus of renovated buildings houses high tech companies. Under Armor, who came here as a start up, now owns the site. For years, industrial uses dominated the waterfront, making it off limits to residents. Now this waterfront is active again and open to all.

1   The tidewater of the Chesapeake

Awards

2003
National Design Merit
Award / American Society
of Landscape Architects

2002
Design Excellence
Award / AIA Maryland,
Juried Exhibition

The Physical Fitness
of Cities / Winter
Olympics, Salt Lake City

2001
Maryland Smart Growth
Award / Tide Point
Office Waterfront Park

2001
Baltimore Heritage
Preservation Society Award

a

b

c

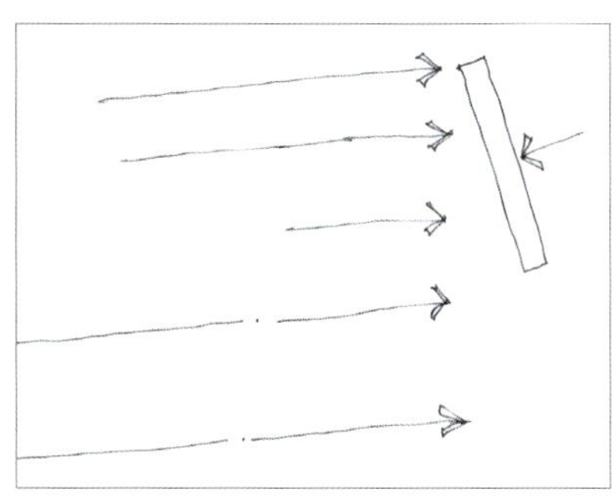

2   Concrete paving lifts to become seating, retaining an industrial palette

d

a   The shifting concrete paving
b   flows over the surface
c   and is extruded into steps
d   the promenade seems to have floated in with the tides

3   The promenade and gangway access with full fog

Extending the Community

Baltimore's gritty Locust Point community used to stop short of the water at the railroad tracks that looped between the rowhouses and the fenced factories. Now the site is open to all.

At the new campus, pedestrian access from the upland became primary as did creating a gathering space at the water. N. Haubert Street now continues from the neighborhood through the site to the water, but cars are stopped short to reserve the harbor edge for pedestrians. As the terrain slopes ten feet down to the water, the rail trestles at either edge of the site maintain their elevation and are preserved as pedestrian harbor overlooks.

Range of Spaces and Uses

A series of places of varying scales create flexible spaces for events or everyday use. The centerpiece is a wood promenade over 300 feet long, a pier in the landscape, with one of the world's longest fog machines. Tall ships can pull alongside, but usually the view is open. Adjacent is a large plaza for events. Smaller gardens with existing site features create unique places to access the buildings or spill out to sit. The largest of these, the "industrial garden," houses the concrete remains of a collection of tanks.

Uses from the water side were also considered. A kayak launch and water taxi stop provide access to the other more populous side of the harbor.

5   Overscale concrete steps flow down towards the waterfront

4   Pedestrian access to the waterfront between the existing buildings

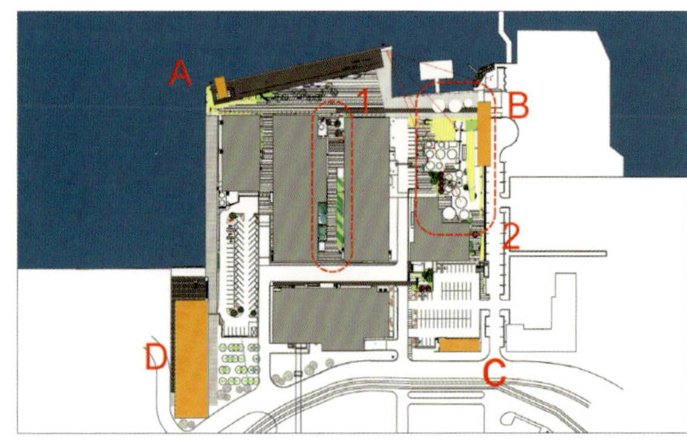

a

a   Master plan for amenity buildings
(A,B,C,D) and artist installations (1,2)

b   Proposed cantilevered Restaurant
B at Hull St overhanging the
promenade, looking west

c   Glassy amenity buildings
as glowing landmarks

d   Stacked office building D
looking south from trestle walk

e   Nightime view of Folly A
with projections—a landmark
visible all around the harbor

d

b

c

e

Tide Point Collaborations

Enrique Norten

Due to the remote location of the site at the outer reaches of the Locust Point neighborhood, the campus required amenities for the convenience of the office workers and community members enjoying the water's edge. Enrique Norten worked with us on a master plan for the site to include these amenities and to provide for future office expansion. He imagined glassy cantilevered structures in contrast to the historic brick factory buildings, one placed on each corner of the site. These structures not only provided the required functions, but also gave a strong identity to the site, especially from the harbor, where it was most visible. In consultation with the client, each marker developed its own scale and function, from a "folly" to a 150,000 sf office building.

A. The second story addition to the pump house on the site's northwest corner was intended as a beacon, and small immigration museum, projecting images that could be seen from the Inner Harbor, while below visitor's could sit in the shade in a café housed in the renovated pump house.

B. A restaurant cantilevered off the old train trestle marks the terminus of Hull St, a main community corridor, and affords views over the water, while a small coffee bar marked the site entrance.

C. A small coffee shop frames the interface with the community on Hull Street.

D. In the southwest, at the juncture of what would be the main site entrance from a new highway extension (now complete) a new office building and parking garage were to rise.

6   Edge of the promenade overlooking plaza event space looking west

7   Promenade in summer

a   View over promenade

Tide Point Collaborations

Guy Nordenson

The former Proctor and Gamble Plant site, like most harbor edges, had been filled over time. To allow for ships to dock, the interface with the water was reduced to a wall, called a bulkhead. We commissioned a bulkhead report to analyze and investigate the site edges and found the north edge was a timber relieving platform— not solid land at all, though this was indistinguishable at the surface. As our design developed, we chose to reveal this structured land by placing a new elevated "pier" promenade over the platform structure. Our structural engineer, Guy Nordenson, helped us distribute the load of this promenade so that the under structure could remain undisturbed. He also designed the truss for the "gangways" which lead up to the boardwalk, which have become an iconic element of the design.

Project Team

Prime consultant -
Landscape Architecture:
W Architecture and
Landscape Architecture

Client:
Struever Bros,
Eccles and Rouse

Civil Engineering:
Whitney, Bailey,
Cox, Magnani

Artists:
David Hess, Alex Castro

Structural Engineer:
Guy Nordenson

Collaborator:
Enrique Norten

8   Edge of the promenade looking east

b   Access gangway to promenade, looking north

c   View from promenade back to campus

STRUCTURING REUSE AND HISTORY

Every site is defined by multiple histories - natural history, political history, cultural history, and so on. As a temporal register, some of these histories record change over millennia, while some trace more ephemeral phenomena. What these stories from the past have in common is that they leave impressions – clues on the site. We call the intersection of these histories, the accumulation of these clues, "the shape of time".

The shape of time can take many forms. In geology, chronological layers accumulate one on top of the other. Specific events disrupt this pattern, through folding or uplift, bringing evidence of the past to the surface. Erosion further amplifies or erases these contours, enriching the story of a place. Similarly, sites accumulate the traces of human action and intervention over time.

We begin each project by looking for such visible human traces, which help us understand the unique qualities and embodiments of a site. Sites are usually part of larger settlement patterns and studying old maps can help us understand the changes which have taken place and where disruptions have occurred. Sometimes remains of past inhabitations still exist, other times only their geometries may remain, if anything at all. We map the palimpsest of layered impressions to understand their scale and distribution, which may suggest new uses or configurations. Preserving artifacts intact and in situ can help us see change and reveal a site's dynamic nature. Of course, like the writing of history, a site is edited as the design evolves—selected artifacts remain to interact with new forms as part of an introduced or renewed site organization. Artifacts are selected less for their visual appeal or didactic function as relics from the past, than for their potential to inform the shape and use of the site in the present and into the future. Alternatively, the preservation of such artifacts is often part of the given site requirements negotiated with the SHPO (State Historic Preservation Officer) or similar organization. These preservation guidelines often influence the project's overall form. How to connect the site's past to its future is thus a constant source of creative dialogue within our team.

When we entered the Tide Point project in Baltimore, for instance, the civil engineer had produced a site plan that prioritized the automobile, bringing vehicles close to the water's edge and eliminating many of the site's topographic changes and industrial features in order to create parking lots edged by a promenade along the harbor. We fought to preserve a larger waterfront space for public access and recreation. This additionally allowed us to retain the large area of tank bases and connected railway trestle. The resulting industrial garden is now a popular spot for social gathering and other forms of environmental engagement.

At the Museum of Industry, a large crane from the nearby Bethlehem Steel plant was moved to the site as a new entry marker. The extraordinary scale of this industrial relic forms a remarkable contrast to the compact rowhouses across the street. Retaining this scale differential highlights the relationship of the former industrial area to the residential neighborhood. Though moving this and other artifacts to the site is anomalous for our practice, the scalar contrasts provide a unique experience imbued with memory and the palpable presence of the past.

Reusing material elements of the site's past sustain its authentic texture and processes of weathering, helping us to perceive change over time. At DoMa barn, the heavy timber structure and the weathered cladding were kept intact to maintain their ragged edges and grey patina and resulting chiaroscouro. The strong visual contrast with the glass signals its change of use from animal to human habitat, while the cladding acts as a necessary sunscreen. Other examples of material reuse include the cobbles at Harlem Piers Park, found under the parking lot and reused for drainage swales, and the granite blocks removed from the bulkhead as the piers were added, reused for seating in the woodland. At Tide Point, a rugged concrete building foundation wall became an enclosure for parking, helping to screen it from the rest of the site. The space beneath a trestle is transformed into office space. A group of tanks are now a water garden. At St. Patrick's Island in Calgary, the wood decking on a demolished bridge will become the cladding of the maintenance facility. Reusing materials sustains site memory and history, while also providing the economic and ecological benefits of recycling resources.

Artists have also been a critical part of this interpretation of collective memory, as have local historians. David Hess scavenged industrial elements from inside the buildings at Tide Point and brought them to the exterior in the form of benches. Alex Castro worked with the existing tank bases and added other concrete elements to focus attention on this aspect of the site. Nari Ward recorded community memories of the West Harlem area and posted them like poetry on traffic bumpers used to define the former parking area. A history of the site, displayed on three panels, was curated by local historian Eric Washington, under the instruction of the community.

Many voices contribute to a site history. Our wide-ranging interpretation of the site does not script reception, but leaves it open to individual encounter.

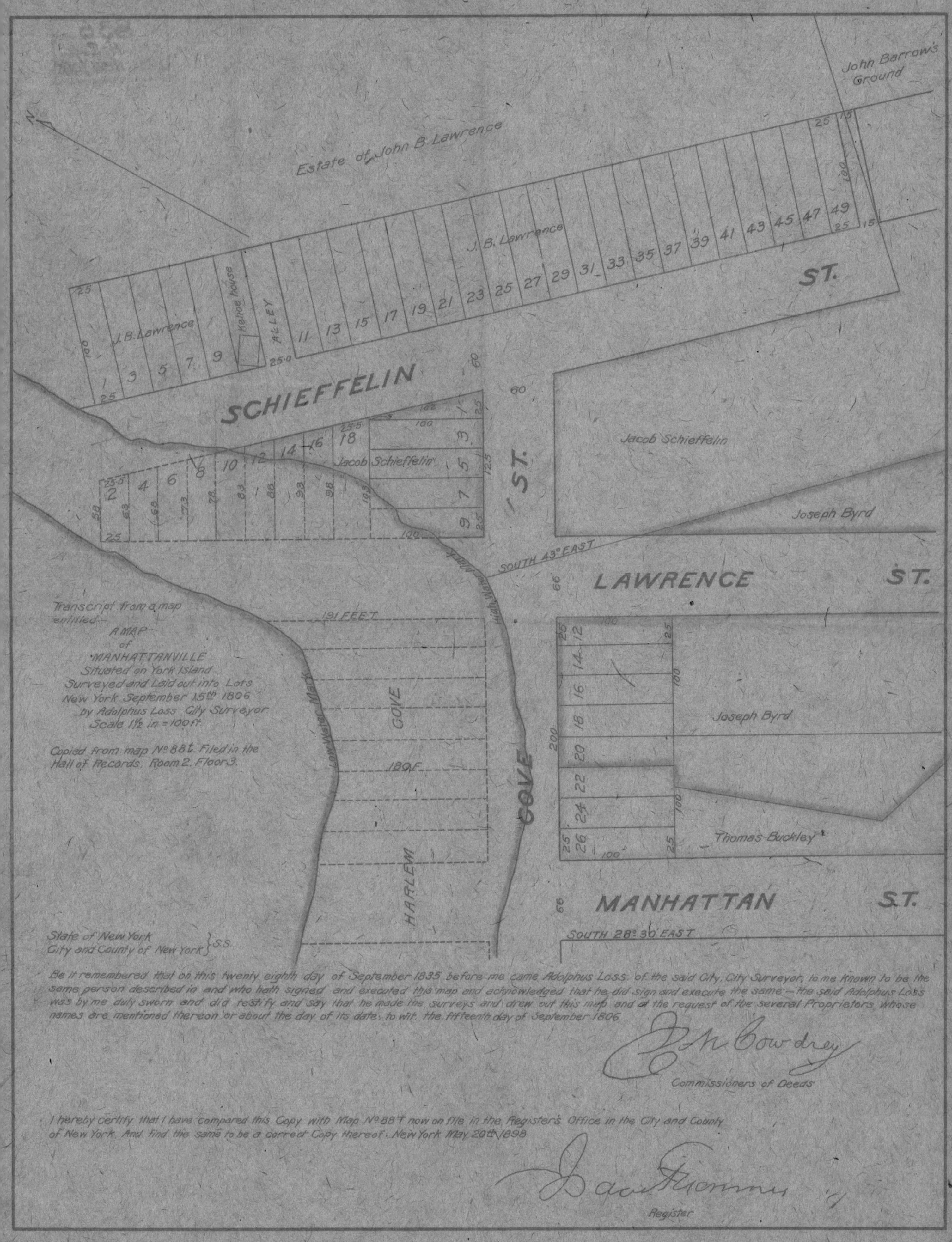

Be it remembered that on this twenty eighth day of September 1835 before me came Adolphus Loss, of the said City, City Surveyor, to me known to be the same person described in and who hath signed and executed this map and acknowledged that he did sign and execute the same — the said Adolphus Loss was by me duly sworn and did testify and say that he made the surveys and drew out this map and at the request of the several Proprietors, whose names are mentioned thereon or about the day of its date, to wit, the fifteenth day of September 1806.

C. N. Cowdrey
Commissioners of Deeds

I hereby certify that I have compared this Copy with Map No. 88 t now on file in the Register's Office in the City and County of New York. And find the same to be a correct Copy thereof. New York May 20th 1898

Isaac Flemmi
Register

BALTIMORE MUSEUM OF INDUSTRY

The Baltimore Museum of Industry wished to expand its program to the outdoors. The Museum houses interactive exhibits and artifacts that tell the industrial history of Baltimore. Situated in a former oyster cannery, the museum is also the terminus of the 7 1/2 mile waterfront promenade. The outdoor expansion would act as a park for the end of the promenade, provide additional programming and a more notable entryway for the museum, and provide parking.

Museum programming was an integral part of the scope and we worked closely with the Museum Director and Exhibit Designers to align with exhibit themes and concepts. The resulting design includes three levels of artifact interpretation—using vertical space to sort the artifacts, creating a kind of timeline. This design system both helps to organize these artifacts and aids in their interpretation. Connection of the site to the Bay is also a part of the educational message—including the importance of improving water quality.

At grade level, are the buildings and surroundings (train tracks, etc) that existed on the site in the past and have been left in place.

Elevated from the existing grade are historic artifacts that have been transported to the site from other portside industries.

Recreated or artistic interpretations of the historic nature of the site, including a sculpture by Baltimore artist David Hess and an open "train shed" style pavilion, are located towards the water where they welcome visitors from the water taxi stop. These interpretive artifacts occupy the topmost vertical layer.

Below these constructed layers, the actual soil and ground of the site are exposed as visitors approach the harbor. Surface water flows off the paved parking and plaza areas into an open, planted bioswale, which slows its flow as it interacts with and brings water to a native landscape, improving water quality in the harbor and providing habitat.

Project Team

Client:
Baltimore Museum
of Industry

Landscape Architect:
Barbara Wilks

Architect:
Cho, Benn, Holback

Civil Engineer:
Gower Thompson

1   Looking north towards the harbor past the sculpture by David Hess

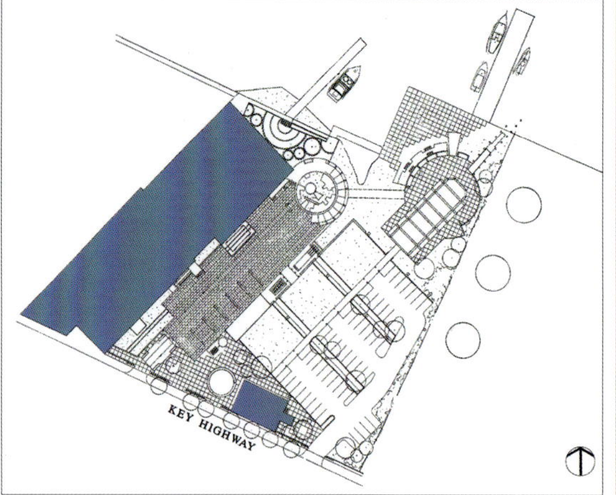

a

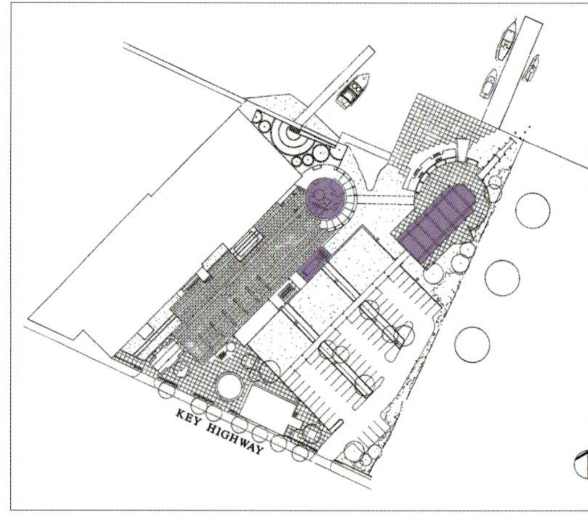

b

1680—Laws of the Indies issued by the Spanish Crown for the American colonies sets guidelines for town development

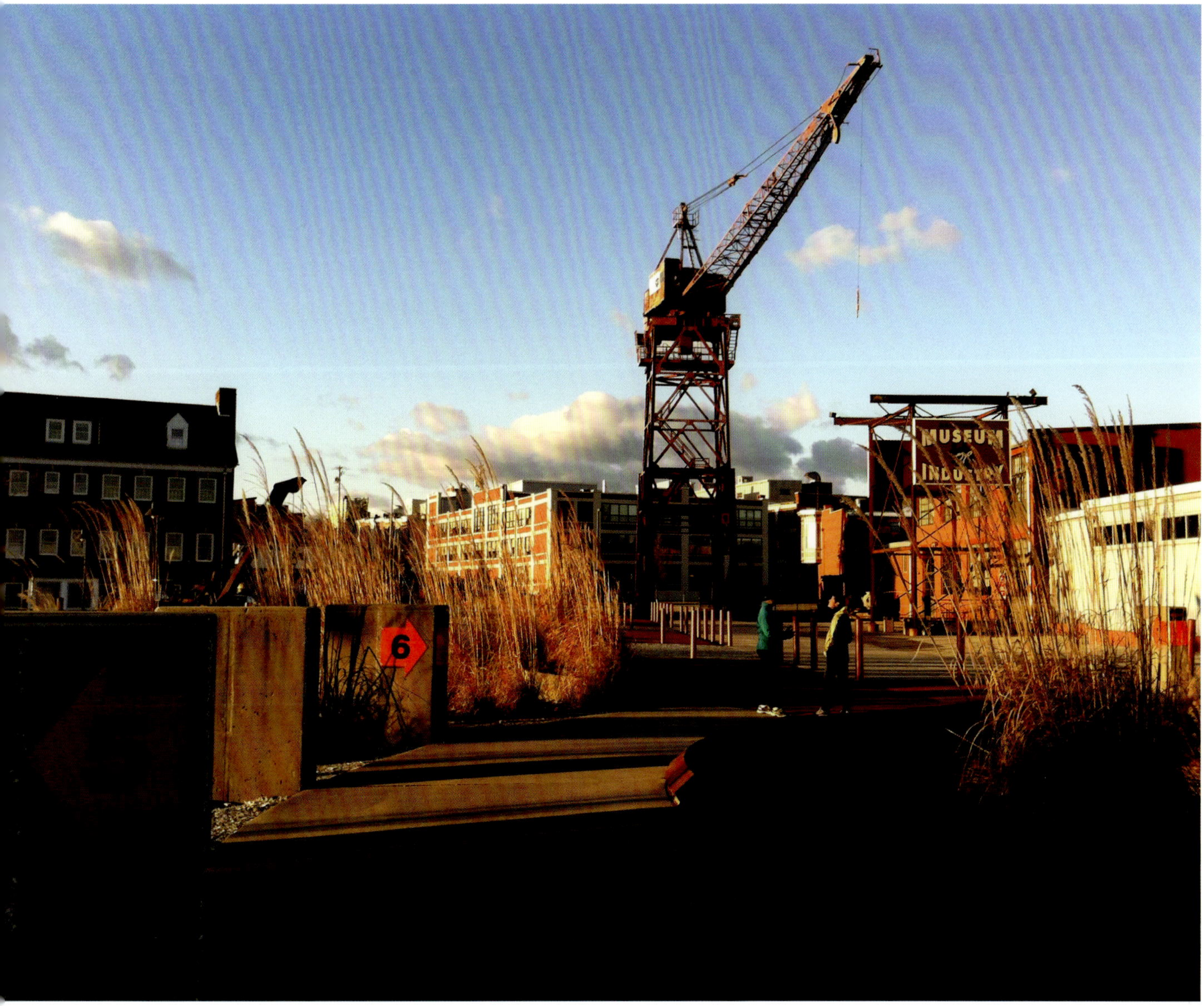

2 Looking south towards the entry plaza and Locust Point neighborhood

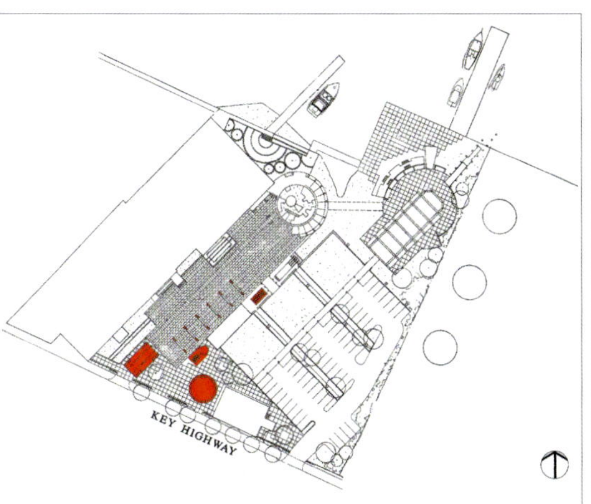

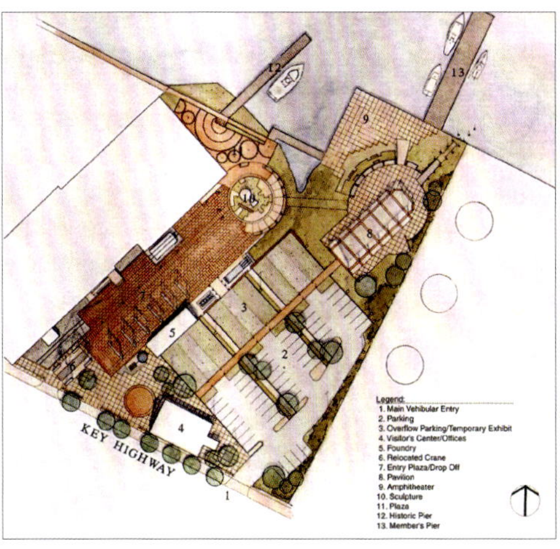

c

d

a Existing site buildings to remain

b Newly constructed site features

c Historic features relocated to the site

d Illustrated site plan

USS CONSTELLATION HERITAGE AND EDUCATION CENTER

The historic frigate, the USS Constellation is situated at the epicenter of the Inner Harbor in Baltimore. Situated alongside Pier One, it is the visual focus of the harbor. As a major tourist attraction however, it lacked a coherent visitor experience, with the existing building blocking views and access to the ship. The new building is a more fitting entry to the ship and gateway to the National Historic Seaport. Our scope of work includes a master plan for the pier, removal of existing building, flood protection, and universal accessibility.

Our biggest challenges were to design a structure that would defer to the historic ship in terms of presence and visibility, meet the client's programmatic and budgetary needs, and satisfy City approvals for this prominent institution at the center of the Inner Harbor.

The proposed project is a one story long rectangular structure. The prefab frame sits directly on the existing pier structure without requiring further reinforcement and creates a building of similar footprint to the existing. We moved the building footprint further away from the ship though to allow passage and views alongside.

The museum experience takes visitors through the center, where they learn about the ship's history, and onto the vegetated roof where they can access the ship and view the Inner Harbor. Iconic translucent bulkheads enclosing the stairs extend through the roof allowing light and people to travel between the museum and ship, highlighting their movement.

Additional improvements were made to ensure the safety and sustainability of the ship and museum. The design and elevated plaza allow the museum to rise above the 100 year flood plain. The green roof lessens storm water runoff and the deck provides space for events, as well as ship access.

Project Team

Client:
Living Classrooms
Foundation

MEP Engineers:
Altieri Sebor Wieber LLC

Structural Engineers:
Robert Silman Associates

Civil Engineers:
RK&K

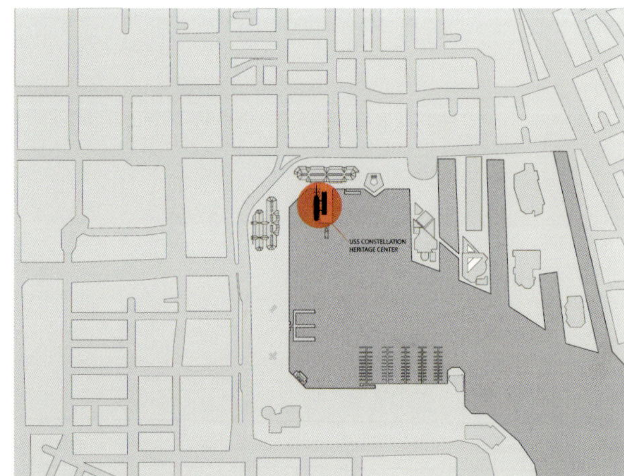

a

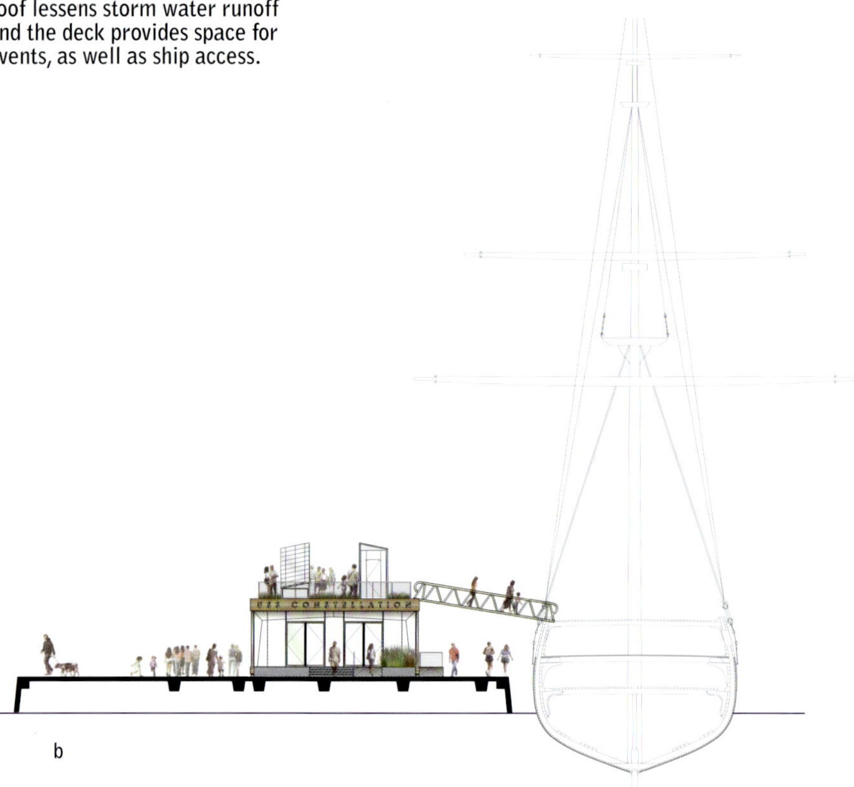

b

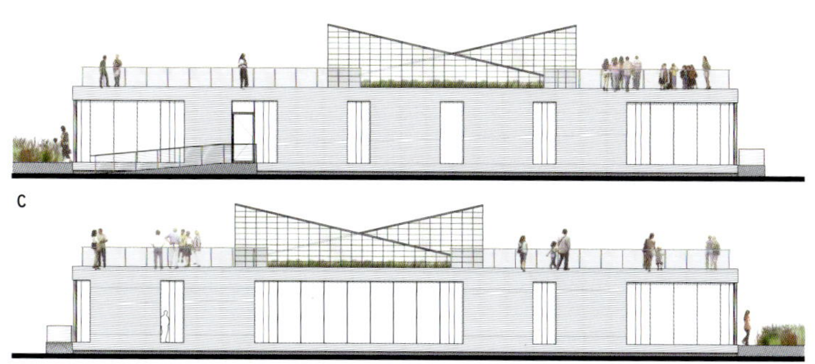

1   View of new visitor center from Harborplace

c

d

a   Site location at harbor center

b   Section through Pier One

c   West elevation

d   East elevation

PIEDMONT — BALTIMORE

The Coastal Plain and the foothills of the Appalachian Mountains meet at a key geological component of the East Coast — the Atlantic Seaboard Fall Line. Because of the desirability of a river port leading to the ocean and a ready supply of water power, many cities including Baltimore were founded where the geological boundary of hard metamorphosized rock meets the sandy outwash of the coastal plain.

1   The foothills of the Appalachian
Mountains in Maryland

2   The foothills in Baltimore, Maryland

CLIPPER MILL

The Clipper Mill complex is positioned just upstream of the fall line, north of the center of the city, where the Jones Falls flows over the rocky hills heading down to the harbor. The client envisioned transforming this collection of structures into a diverse mixed use community.

The primary goal of the site plan and the landscape design is to create linkages between and among the existing buildings and the various new uses, new buildings to the existing structures, and the site as a whole to its inherent topography, ecology, and history.

Scale was a major consideration here. The site is oriented along a single street that curves uphill into a large and heavily forested city park. On the downhill side of the street against the forest were two huge industrial buildings: these giant buildings were retained intact, with a new condo building situated adjacent. These larger buildings were planned for residential use. On the uphill side of the street away from the forest, was a variety of longer, lower buildings which had aggregated over time. These, smaller, more idiosyncratic buildings were planned for commercial use.

We connected these variously aged structures with outdoor common spaces and plantings, creating a lively series of intimate interconnected places that balance the weight of the industrial relics across the street. Past these clusters of activity, almost where the road disappears into the forest, a community of new "green" homes is nestled into the hill and among the trees.

The landscape supports the structure of these linkages, helps to reinforce the industrial character of the site (it has historic certification), and seeks to preserve and encourage the ecology of the land and of the people living and working there. Tree species from the adjacent forest are continued down through the site, and the existing mill stream flows right through one of the buildings. Storm water is filtered and managed by bioswales and permeable pavements. Industrial relics are used throughout—most memorably columns that were metal replicas or models for columns used in the Capital, which help to define the verticality of a pool area, designed by artist Alex Castro.

Project Team

Client:
Struever Bros, Eccles, and Rouse, Inc

Architect:
Cho, Benn, Holback

Landscape Architect:
W Architecture and Landscape Architecture LLC

Civil Engineer:
Gower Thompson

Pool feature:
Alex Castro

1   New public space allows people to flow between the interior and the exterior

2   Seating space looking back towards renovated restaurant interior, artisan studios above

a   Before view of site

b   After view showing fire pit fabricated from industrial remnant

a

b

DOMA BARN

Two private art collectors were in the midst of transforming their rural estate — a historic farm in Baltimore County — into a place to entertain and display their growing collection. The restored historic house was perched overlooking the valley, but its beautifully scaled intimate rooms did not always accommodate the scale of contemporary art. The largest of a series of outbuildings was a historic bank barn with weathered slats sitting on a stone foundation wall. The client wished to use it as a larger more flexible space to exhibit works of contemporary art and to gather friends. Ancillary programs include an eat-in kitchen, guest quarters, office, and storage space.

We were struck at once by the ever changing quality of light coming through the gaps in the deteriorating barn siding. Our solution was to preserve the existing timber barn structure, retaining the weathered cladding as a sunscreen, while a glass volume inserted within it highlights the art collection, the surrounding historic structure, and opens to the landscape beyond. To preserve the spatial scale of the barn, the volume remains open. Rooms which required enclosure were gathered in a single central core which rises through the two levels and terminates in an open study overlooking the space from the eves. Stacked 1x3 pine boards form the mass of the enclosure. Though we left the barn siding in its decayed state, it was coated with preservative to prevent further deterioration.

Even art collectors have budgets, though. Originally, we worked with a construction manager, but the 60% cost estimate came in too high. In response, we went through a round of value engineering replacing curtain wall with a standard window wall system, limiting the extent of glass and creating more easily constructible connections between the barn and glass structure. With traditional design-bid-build and standard glass systems and materials, the winning bid came in exactly on budget.

1   View from historic farmhouse

Awards

2004
National Honor Award
American Institute
of Architects

2004
Excellence in
Construction Award
Associated Builders
and Contractors

2003
Design Excellence Award
AIA New York Chapter

1839—rubber processing invented by Charles Goodyear

2   View from the upper lawn looking into main space of the barn

3   View from the lower level terrace with stairs to the main level

4   Top of the stairs, in the porch space

Doma Barn Collaborations

Nat Oppenheimer

Material properties contribute to the visual effect of a project, but their inherent structural properties also affect how they can be put together. Wood is a structural member that moves and even "creeps", that is deforms from a constant load bearing over time. Glass by comparison is relatively brittle, even though it too slowly deforms through the pull of gravity. To set a glass box inside a heavy timber structure, which is prone to moving with the winds and the weather, you need a structural engineer who is sensitive to the aesthetics of renovation, as well as the material differences of wood, steel, aluminum, and glass. Robert Silman Associates and Nat Oppenheimer in particular is such an engineer. Nat created minimally invasive ways to stiffen the barn, preserving its cladding while repairing its structure and creating a more plumb presence. Steel angles unite the wood connections, limiting movement, and stainless steel cables limit racking. The result is an almost invisible yet effective marrying of the structural systems.

Tom McCracken

Working on a barn which is about to fall to ruin, and keeping it intact while you thread another structure inside requires a special patience and understanding of historic buildings. Henry Lewis Contractors had worked on many historic structures including Thomas Jefferson's Monticello and the Basilica in Baltimore, so I knew we were in good hands, but our expectations were even exceeded by their diligence and interest in every detail. At one point after a heavy rainfall, the stone wall washed out from under the barn, but due to their foresight in shoring up the timbers, the structure remained standing. When original materials are irreplaceable, having this type of foresight in the contractor not only affects the final result, but avoids potential catastrophic loss. This sensitivity pervades the smallest detail, showing a respect for the materials old and new as they are brought together.

a

5   View of glass enclosure over space of old addition

b

c

Project:
Client:
Stanley Mazaroff/
Nancy Dorman

Architect:
W Architecture
and Landscape
Architecture, LLC

General Contractor:
Henry H. Lewis
Contractors, LLC

Structural Engineer:
Robert Silman
Associates, PC

Mechanical Electrical
Engineers:
Spears/ Votta Associates

Civil Engineer:
Gower Thompson Inc.

Interior Designer:
Johnson/Berman

a   Lower level bedroom

b   View from dining area
towards core and stair

c   Lower level bedroom
looking out to terrace

d   Building plans: Lower level,
first and loft

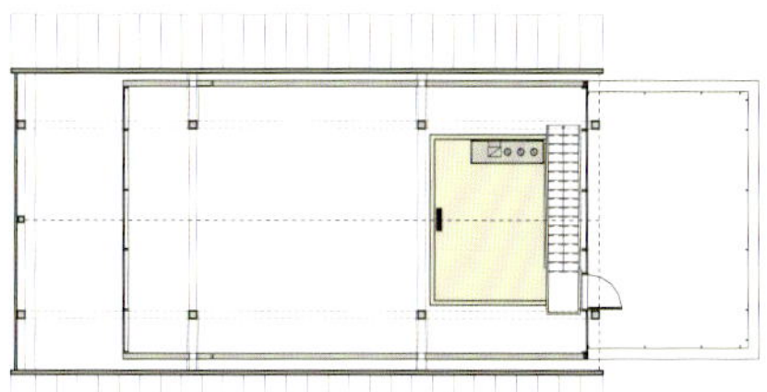

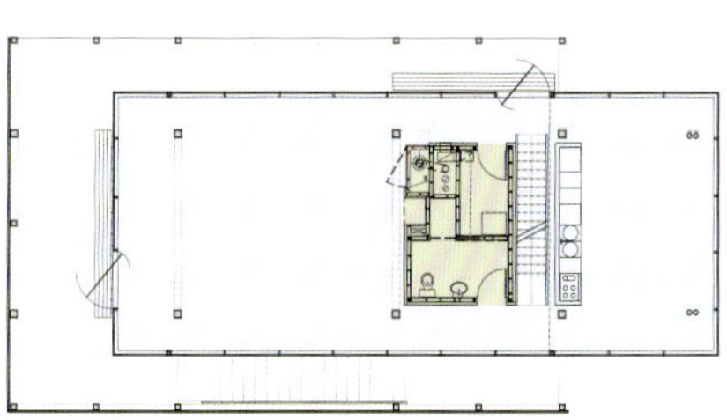

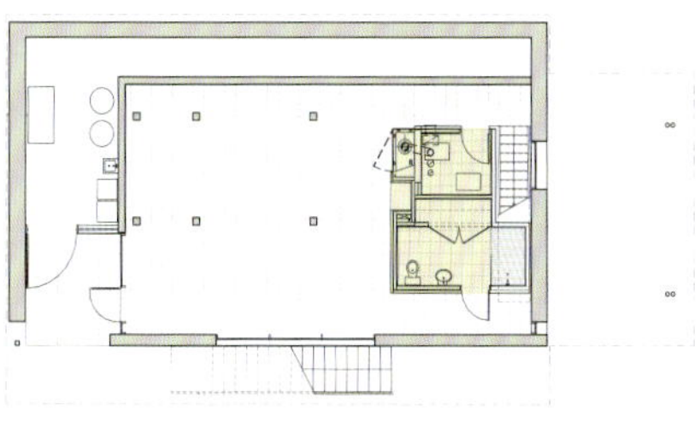

d

6   View of barn interior

1872—Yellowstone established as our first National Park

STRUCTURING USE AND EXPERIENCE

Understanding how individuals, families and communities structure and inhabit their own particular cultural and social worlds is critical to creating places that will become meaningful. Many powerful and poignant stories emerge during our site investigations. Reading a site through the multiplicity of these stories, as well as through community expressions of hope and concern, gives us insight into connecting uses and places in ways that will resonate. Our goal is to use design to build consensus and understanding of new ways to engage with the changing world around us.

As patterns of human use change, abandoned sites often become isolated and disconnected from the fabric of a neighborhood, a family, a citizen. New connections and uses are necessary to reintegrate these fragments back into the structure of a place at multiple scales. Many of the examples in this book are former industrial sites, which by nature were closed to the public and connected to wholly different transportation, service and social structures. Others are underutilized places in need of reinvention. Much of our design process is dedicated to working to reintegrate these sites into the social and physical fabric and to find uses which reactivate them and encourage engagement.

Fostering engagement begins in the planning process. To create a place that will be embraced by the people for whom the design is intended, their ranging concerns must be acknowledged. Listening to the aspirations and needs of the diversity of potential users is an active and iterative process requiring mediated exchange and inspired engagement. We look for methods and means to address community needs in flexible yet compatible ways, as well as propose new ways of seeing and addressing challenges that might not be obvious. For the West Harlem Piers project, we met with representatives from over 40 community organizations, city agencies, and other groups monthly for a year. Together, a consensus developed on the use for the valley district as a whole, as well as the specific city-owned site at the water's edge. As discussions progress, when alternatives are vetted and choices and tradeoffs become clear, a consensus usually starts to emerge.

It is also important to sustain engaged momentum throughout the design process. In West Harlem, resident input shifted as we switched from the master-planning phase to the site implementation phase. This was not a reflection of collective indecision, but more the result of a changing focus of the inquiry. As we began the park implementation, the community remained engaged in the actual design and our conceptual master plan for the park was modified substantially, as their focus shifted to this site alone. The view down 125th St became a primary point of concern — where we had initially placed the piers, the community wanted the water left open as an unobstructed river view. As the piers and boating activity were moved to either side of the street-end view, a stronger plan emerged, based on community feedback.

The choreography of a place—the sequence of events and their physical manifestation, creates an experience. Finding the right synergies between places and uses which create experiences rather than unrelated program areas, leads to engagement and stewardship. The choreography of the past and the future, or the new and the old, can lead to new experiences. At the DoMa Barn for instance, where one enters between the new glass structure and the old barn slats, the light creates a unique and ever changing experience. At Tide Point, the remaining industrial circular concrete tank bases interrupt the linear landscape in an provocative way, and at St Patrick's Island, the creation of new water channels from areas of fill increases the "islandness" of the place, and the opportunity to interact safely with the water—a new experience.

The unfolding order of activities in a park, how they relate to points of entry and to each other, are also critical. At St. Patrick's Island in Calgary, the site diagram depicted a beaded necklace with larger beads at the two ends and another big one in the center - as three areas for concentrated human use. Thus nodes of activity encourage entry into the park, but once inside, a visitor has the opportunity to pass through different ecological environments where human activity is limited. This ensures a richly experiential yet also functional landscape. As single use spaces often sit vacant, places which can accommodate a variety of overlapping programs are best where land is scarce. Providing pier space for fishing at many waterfront sites also offers visitors the opportunity to get out over the water. Water features provide interactive elements for children to play as well as

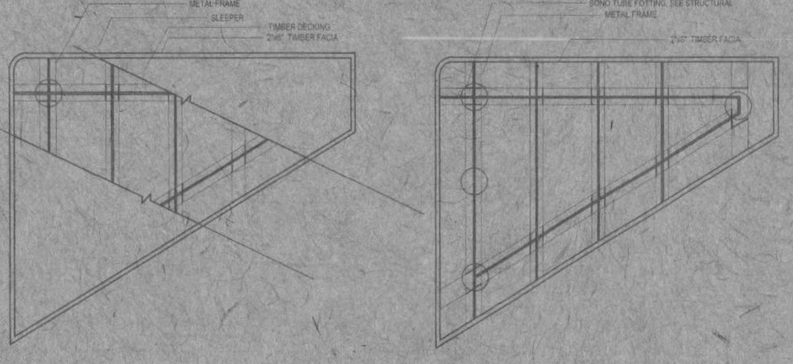

St. Patricks Island platform seating

others to watch, engaging varying ages without relegating youngsters to fenced and isolated enclosures. Water features can also be turned off, so that the space can be put to other temporary uses, like a small festival, as with our design for the Troy Riverfront amphitheater. These juxtapositions can also lead to novel hybrid programs.

Another method for generating public interest, engagement and future stewardship is organizing temporary participatory community events on site. Public spaces should accommodate and even encourage a calendar of individual and community rituals, both temporary and permanent. For instance, we organized a "Bioblitz" (when an ecologist works with the community to identify the diversity of species on a site) at St. Patrick's Island in Calgary before construction even began. While the results were enlightening for us as we developed our planting design, the activity, most primarily, inspired public enthusiasm and awareness about the island, its resources and the potential for its future experience as a "living island".

In terms of site design, seating is one of the most critical components of a successful public space. Seating has the potential to generate new patterns of socialization and gathering – it offers a place to talk with a friend or a group of friends or adjacent strangers, a place to sit and watch others, a place to have a picnic, to sunbathe, to read, and so on, in any combination. Seating can happen on a bench, a platform, on stairs. Its relation to pathways is of critical importance, as well as what is situated behind or in front. We also observe the locations people sit after we complete a project—something as simple as a misplaced bench can impact the feel of a whole design. When we presented our Schematic Design to the Advisory Board for St Patrick's Island, their main comment had to do with provision of seating. They encouraged us to work harder to make each of the destinations be more welcoming. In the following Design Development phase we did just that, crafting both the contours of the space and the elements within it to make a related family of spaces, that together with the landscape created vastly different experiences.

Places continue to evolve after we leave. After a project is built, we learn more about human nature and dynamics of public space by returning to assess how the site is used—often in ways we had never planned. Children take delight in discovering opportunistic spaces for play, and will invent games which incorporate elements imagined for other purposes. We hear stories of a hawk who has found a special perch in one of our parks or how the relation of a grocery store to a resting spot has spawned a new picnic area for the community. Though in my 40 years of listening I have heard many similar stories about communities' attachments to or aspirations for a place, our particular solution for each site is always different. Reaching a particular design synthesis that integrates both social needs and optimized ecological performance is what inspires me to continue making public spaces in the city. A sustainable place integrates community vision, but is inevitably not what anyone expected when the project began. We feel a design is truly successful if it fosters new and more sustainable relationships among people and between people and the natural forces and rhythms that shape a place. The experience of the place itself becomes its most memorable activity.

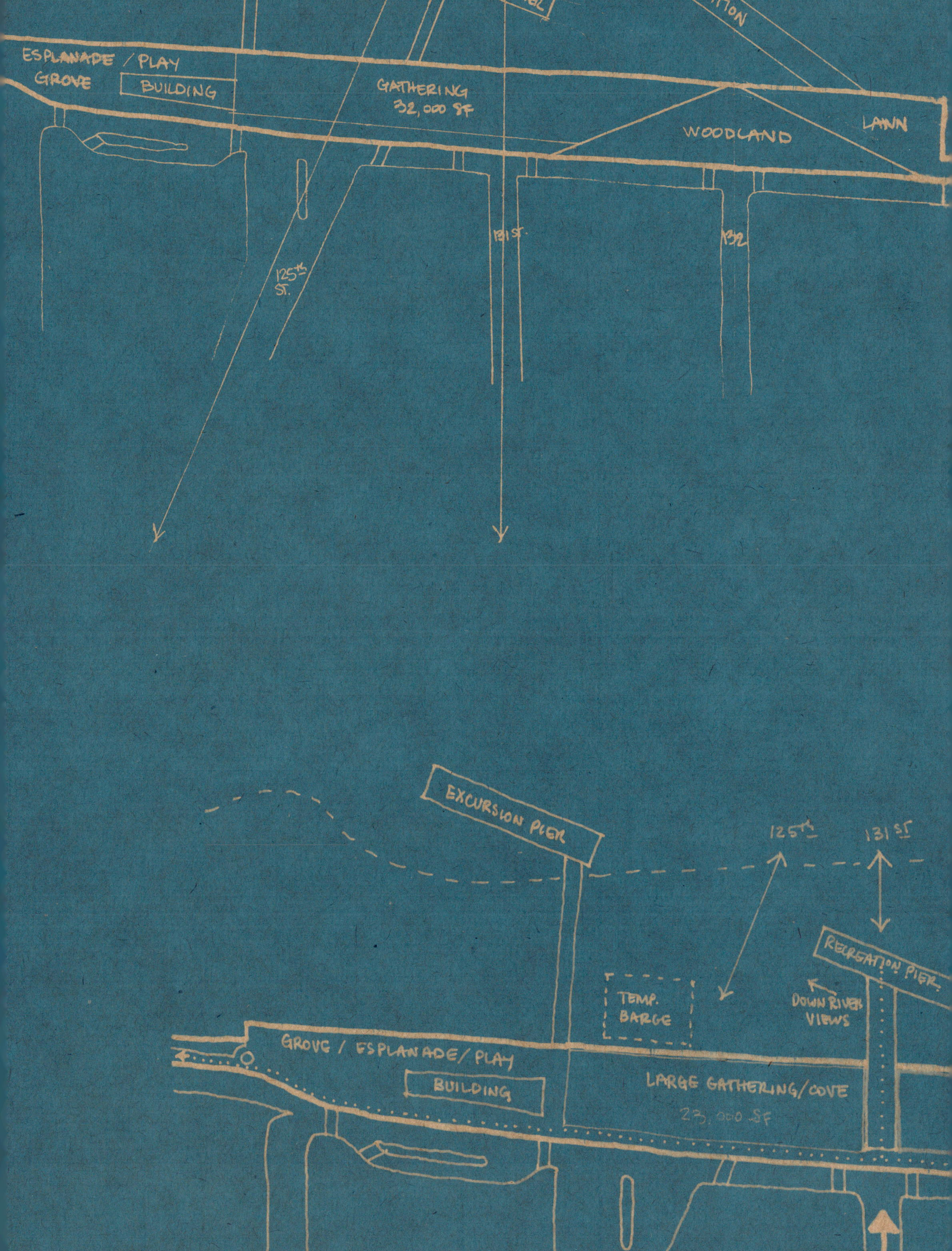

ESPLANADE / PLAY
GROVE
BUILDING
GATHERING
32,000 SF
WOODLAND
LAWN
125th ST.
131 ST
132
EXCURSION PIER
125th
131 ST
RECREATION PIER
TEMP. BARGE
DOWN RIVER VIEWS
GROVE / ESPLANADE / PLAY
BUILDING
LARGE GATHERING / COVE
23,000 SF

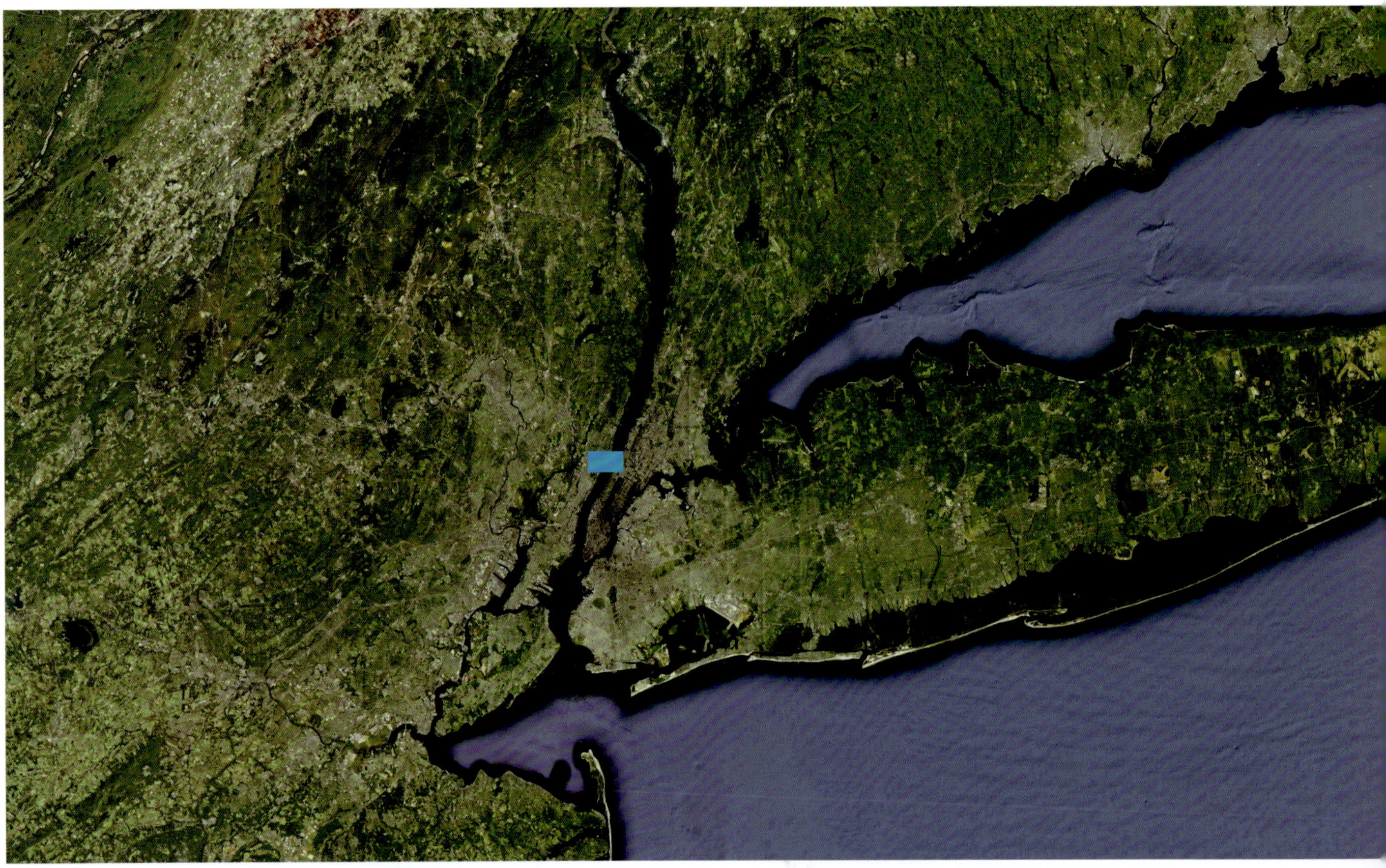

HUDSON ESTUARY — NYC

"We live in a time not of mainstream but of many streams, or even, if you insist upon a river of time, then we have come to delta, maybe even beyond delta to an ocean which is going back to the skies."

John Cage, KPFA radio 1992

1   Hudson River Estuary and the Long Island Sound

2   New York City with the Hudson and Harlem Rivers

WEST HARLEM PIERS PARK

Master Plan

Working for the New York City Economic Development Corporation, the goal for the West Harlem Master Plan was to create a plan for this area where Harlem's "main street" meets the Hudson. Specifically the NYCEDC wanted to begin a community process to inform the use of a city-owned waterfront parcel, which had been in long term "temporary" use as a parking lot. Creating a vision that could bring together the owners of the site, the community desires for their quickly changing neighborhood, and the various federal, state, and local agencies having jurisdiction, was the challenge. We assembled a working group of over 40 representatives from stakeholders, community groups, and agencies, and over a six month period discussed and debated economic, transportation, and land use issues to create consensus on a new vision for the area and use for the site—a park that would anchor the neighborhood's emerging identity. Creating this park was the first phase of the plan; proceeding phases would make additional transportation linkages, and then land use and zoning changes to foster economic development.

Phase One Implementation:

The Park

Our mission for the West Harlem Piers Park was to turn a narrow parking lot (the width of a tennis court) into both a community park and a regional node on the West Side bike path along the Hudson. On such a narrow site, this was a challenge. Our initial design ideas also grappled with how to connect this important access point to the river and its specific location and history, though no historic elements remained.

The area is a natural cove among hills which had lead to its early settlement and urbanization. We based our design on the idea of the cove form as a place of collection. The diagonal, organic patterns of driftwood deposition in a cove help to visually orient the site in a way that de-emphasized its narrowness. We also increased its actual size by working with the Department of Transportation to reclaim over 45,000 sf from the adjacent roadway for the park and biketrail—half the size of the existing site!

We wanted the site to be anchored in its cultural history as well as its ecological identity. The site's recent past as a parking lot with its chain link fence and concrete bulwarks along the water provided few outlets for community use, but it had remained a popular fishing spot. And for many years before that the cove had been a landing place for boats. The West Harlem Piers Park retains venues for fishing and for boating.

1   Seating in the main cove gathering space

Project Team

Prime Consultant Landscape Architect, Architect: W Architecture and Landscape Architecture

Client: New York City Economic Development Corporation

Economic Advisor: Ernst and Young

Transportation: Sam Schwartz Engineering

Artist: Nari Ward

Marine and Civil Engineers: DMJM/Harris

Graphics: Port City Studios

Irrigation: Northern Design

Historic Curator: Eric K. Washington

Landscape Contractor: Trocom Construction Corp.

2   Diagonal forms expand the space

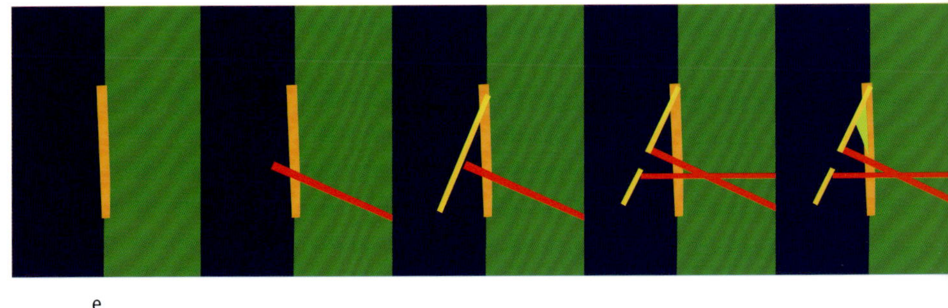

e

3   Water feature situated between the dunes at the intersection of 133rd St.

a

b

c

4 The promenade edge

A variety of additional programming is integrated into the park through overlapping layers. Small but critical changes in vertical elevation help to sort and separate these spaces creating a wide diversity of places within the park, and allowing a wide range of people to use the park in many different ways concurrently.

The cultural history of the park was further integrated into the design through the artwork of Nari Ward, an internationally renowned local artist. For its many years as a parking lot the fisherman were the sole recreational users of the land, a continuous connecting thread all the way through the park's history to before the island's settlement by the Dutch. This fragile connective cultural tissue is the foundation Nari Ward's artwork "Voices" that is part of the park's design.

Aspects of the site's other histories are brought together through reuse of existing historic materials. Closer inspection revealed that some artifacts did remain—not all had been erased. Cobblestones that had been covered up by the asphalt parking lot were salvaged and reused as swales to channel surface water flow. The historic granite blocks which formed the bulkhead that separated the land and the water were left intact, and where the new piers were added and the blocks were removed, we reused them for seating in the woodland.

d

a Cobbles found under the parking lot

b Cobbles reused as drainage swales

c Plan of park

d Pathway at edge between woodland and cove

e Diagram of site development – the site, 125th st., the pier, street connections, the woodland anchor

SPEED
LIMIT
50

5   Diagonals expand the space. Topography separates woodland and cove

6   The cove

West Harlem Piers
Park Collaboration

Alex Washburn

Alex Washburn comes by urban design naturally. A student of history like his father, Alex sees the world in terms of the *longue duree,* combining the social, the economic, and the political. The master plan for the West Harlem Area owes a great deal to his input. As a partner in W at the time, his influence is seen in the three pronged approach for implementation strategy to the detail of the ginkgo leaf as the selected tree for 125th Street streetscape (linking its arched leaf shape to the historic viaducts spanning the area). In addition to the West Harlem plan, our work included many community plans during his time with us, including projects in Durham, NC; Nashville, Tennessee; Providence, Rhode Island; Seoul, South Korea, and others.

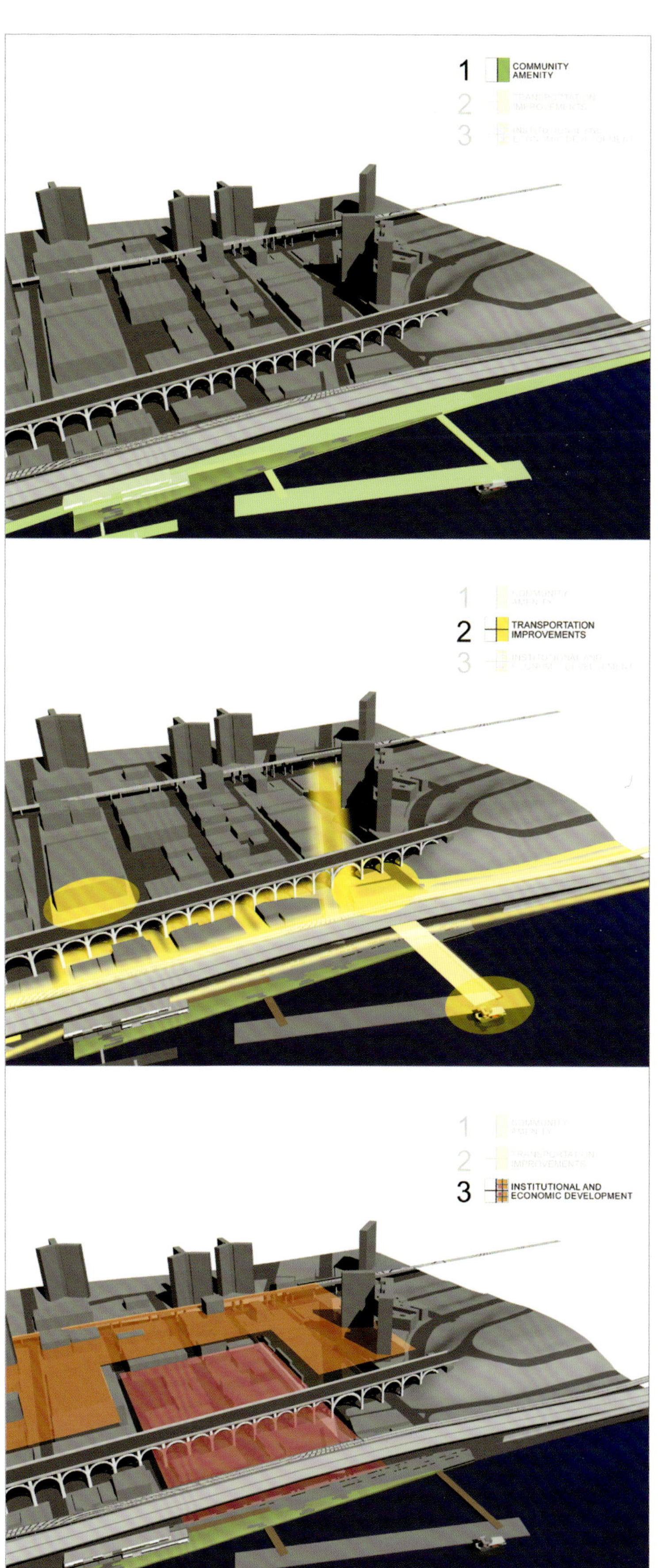

7 Three step master plan

THE EDGE IN WILLIAMSBURG

The Williamsburg waterfront has been dominated by industry and its relics for over a century—making it largely off limits to the public. New zoning is transforming the water's edge by changing use, increasing density, and requiring public access. As landscape architects for both the new residential towers and the public waterfront park, we had the challenge of ensuring that the towers act not as symbolic fences blocking public access but as gateways to the river, shepherding visitors and residents alike to the public spaces that now line the water's edge.

The site encompassed two long narrow blocks at the edge of the North Brooklyn grid. We wanted to emphasize the dynamism of the relationship between the land and the water —between the city and nature— and we began by rethinking the character of the streets which define the site. These dead end streets held little traffic, offering the opportunity for greening and pedestrianization. We use the transitional spaces of these streets to increase the interaction between the city grid and the "park." One street emphasizes the water: it transitions from street, to semi permeable pedestrian space, to grass. All along, it gently slopes to and into the water; it's a direct connection between land and sea, urban and natural. The other street emphasizes the land. A meadow-like bio-swale creates a sense of broadness, and greatly increases the permeability of the water's edge, providing habitat, recreational space, and filtering stormwater.

Between these two streets is the main space of the park, overlooking the water, with a pier for ferry service to Manhattan. This main space is broken up into more intimate and diverse sections with a variety of seating, terraced up the gentle slope and above the partially subterranean parking structure. The grading camouflages the garage and ensures that each seating area has a full view to the water and city beyond.

The Empire Pier is placed on an odd angle, seemingly random, but actually orchestrating a view of the Empire State Building. (It has become a popular spot for film and TV shoots, perhaps for that reason—a Brooklyn pier pointing to the heart of Manhattan.) The extension of that pier visually into the terraced upland emphasizes the porosity of the interchange between water and land by bringing the force of the waterfront deeper into the site.

The dynamic site forms were inspired by the quantities of driftwood accumulating at the site and left by the tidal surging of the East River. Ferry and water taxis use the piers, creating a gateway to the site and the city beyond from the water side and helping people to flow through, and not just to, the site.

1   Phase 1 view from tower

Awards

2012
ASLA NY Chapter
Merit Award
The Edge Park

"Making City" Exhibit at
Rotterdam Biennale, NYC
Department of City Planning
The Edge Park

2008
Ecotones: Mitigating NYC's
Contentious Sites
Center for Architecture

2   View of Empire State Building from the upper terrace

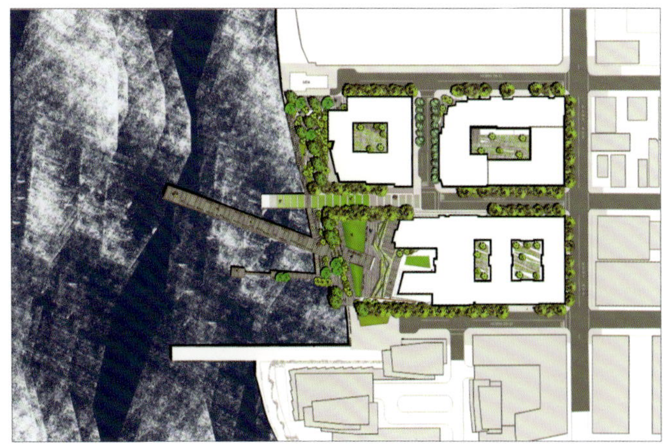

e

 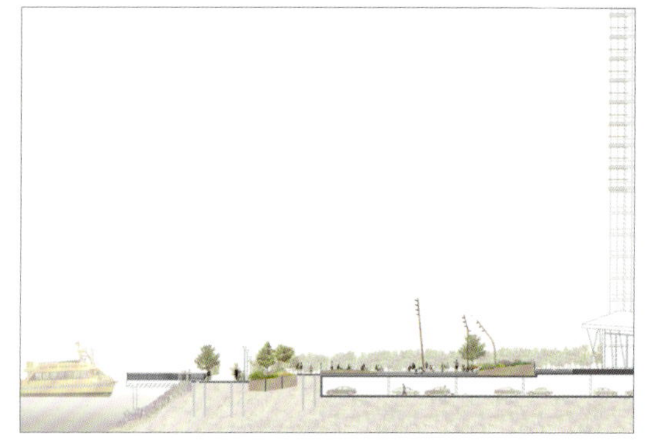 

a   b

3   View down former N 6th St

a   Driftwood collecting at the site prior to construction

b   Section showing relationship to partially buried parking

c   Early sketch of the river edge

d   Early rendering of the river edge

e   Plan with Phase 2, now under construction

c

d

Project Team

Client:
Douglaston Development

Landscape Architect:
W Architecture and
Landscape Architecture LLC

Civil Engineer:
Phillip Habib Associates

Marine/structural
Engineers:
McLaren Engineering Group

Contractor:
Levine Builders

7   Site as a theater to the water

1927—New York Harbor oyster beds closed due to toxicity

STRUCTURING LAND FORM AND MOVEMENT

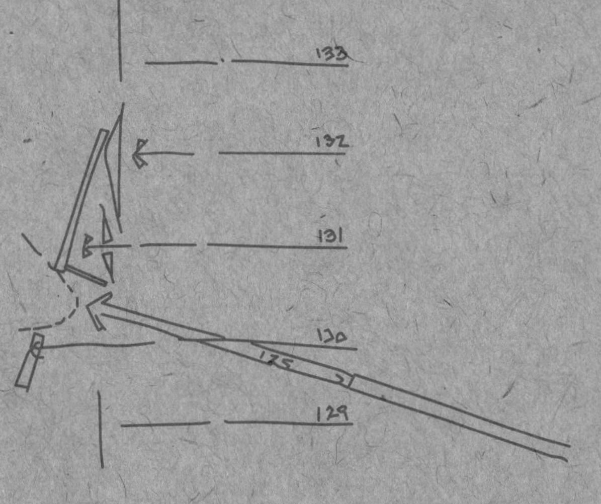

1 Street as diagonal
which breaks the pier

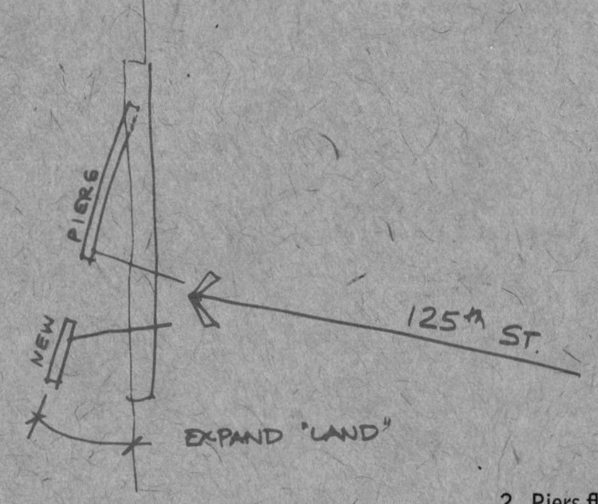

2 Piers float out
like sand bars

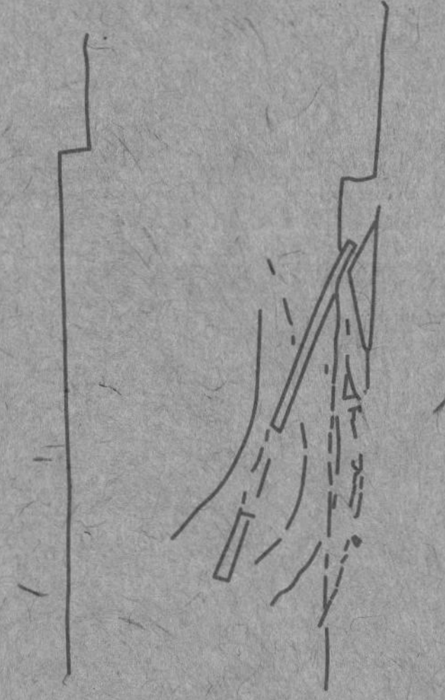

3 Imagined cove
waters flow inward
onto the site,
depositing elements

While sites are dynamic places of change, their geographic location in space remains constant. This situation in space with its underlying geology means sites take on specificity of topography, climate and orientation, which gives rise to particular vegetation, animal life, and a host of other curiosities that make up the recipe for uniqueness. The given conditions of each site are the result of natural processes such as weathering, erosion, material transport and sedimentation. Different geomorphologic processes, from glaciers to uplift to ocean waves, dominate at different spatial and temporal scales to create complex and variant landscapes.

The sites we work on have also been modified by generations of human use. Early settlement patterns are usually a direct result of the particular qualities of a place, high ground, good orientation, a supply of water, etc. Over time: as transportation or other infrastructures and associated use patterns change, disruptions can occur. At the extreme, relationships to surrounding communities and underlying ecologies have been to various extents erased. As we look to change the site and to engage people in the process, we have found that forms which reveal specificities of location and the broader ecosystem help ground people in time and space. Human cognition of the environment subtly relies on such perceptible clues.

For instance, when we started working on waterfronts, the predominate method for connecting isolated areas was extending the city grid onto the site. This provided continuity and access. Yet it also prioritized automobile infrastructure as the impetus for site organization, rather than the physical processes, forms and organizations of the water's edge. Environments impacted by water's forces, such as erosion and sedimentation, can reveal a sort of geologic clarity of material, structure, process and time. Our goal is to ground the site in such latent qualities and then to bring these into a meaningful relationship with human processes and activity.

As we began reshaping our sites on the water, we started to learn from landforms shaped by water. Sedimentation leads to a sorting of material by size. Orientation of forms relate to the direction of water movement. At West Harlem Piers Park, for instance, the key characteristic of the larger planning area was its topographic valley form. The imagined movement of water and the patterns of deposition and erosion, that generated this form became the creative catalyst for the site's new topography. Its subtly sloping dunes orient the site to the water and create a series of diagonal edges which both delineate and link spaces intended for varying activity. Piers float off shore like sand bars. Similarly at The Edge, a waterfront park in Williamsburg Brooklyn, the terracing and orientation of the site towards the water creates a kind of amphitheater — the theatrical focus of which is the river and its backdrop, the Manhattan skyline. This continuous gesture contrasts with the thrust of the pier tossed like driftwood inland onto the site. Here, the interplay of this East River tidal strait, whose water violently changes direction four times a day, influenced the particular geometric character of the forms, as did the dramatic views to the Empire State Building. In contrast, the slow and subtly shifting tides of the upper Chesapeake influence a sort of oscillating field of concrete floating over the surface of the Tide Point site, while the pier rests softly against the edge. Thus the character of each design is embedded in, and responsive to, the processes that have long shaped the site.

Another very different example of this approach is our Mill River competition entry for a park in Stamford, Connecticut. Here, the client desired the river expand beyond its engineered channels to create a more active edge. The client also wanted a pavilion to act as a focal point for the site. Our solution was to create a pavilion in the form of a natural levee — a subtle rise in the land as the river regularly deposits sediment during annual flooding. We positioned it in the landscape to delineate new spaces for programmed activities.

Our sites are meant to invite interaction and discovery — moving across and through varied topography impacts our perception of both space and time. The interplay of forms that define spaces and the movement systems by which we register spatial variety are set in dynamic relationship. Working in both plan and section we are able to choreograph the richness of this experience. We also link movement systems with ecologies of place, such as the fluid dynamics of water. For instance, at St. Patrick's Island in Calgary, the trail system takes on the form of braided streams, offering multiple choices for meandering. Experiencing the topography in a variety of loops of different scales entices expanded exploration of the site and increased interaction with other visitors. The specific frequency and temporal meter of the intersections endows each path with a unique rhythmic character. The diagonal system at West Harlem Piers Park expands the narrow space both socially and visually by providing thickened edges for

inhabitation. In another example, the field of concrete at Tide Point dissolves pathways to inspire free movement.

As these water-inspired forms meet the street grid, we introduce special design features. At West Harlem, small connector bridges to the piers are extensions of the street grid sidewalks pulled out to the water. The centerlines of 33rd and 35th streets locate the water feature and the woodland apex respectively. These special features act as gateways to the site from the city. At the Museum of Industry, as well as the Edge in Williamsburg, the street extension becomes the main entry plaza connecting the community to the water.

Public places of the 21st century are a blend of the cultural and ecological. Uniting urban programs with landforms that perform ecologically and enrich movement experience heighten awareness of the forces and rhythms that shape the world around us.

Evidence Revealed

Many of the landscapes in this book were formed by glaciers.
New York City marks the southernmost boundary of an
ice sheet that mantled much of North America, covering
our projects in Alberta, Ohio, upstate NY and NYC and
the Chesapeake. The Laurentide Ice Sheet advanced and
retreated over a period of 60,000 years. The last advance
11,000 years ago, the Wisconsin glaciations, extended
from Alberta to the East Coast. These glaciers literally
created many of the landscapes we see today. The Finger
Lakes region in NY, the terminal moraine deposits in
south western Ohio, and the Hudson River estuary in
NYC all still show the effects and evidence of glaciers.

In New York City, the glaciers carved out the landscape
of the region. As the glaciers melted and receded, glacial
meltwater created huge lakes between the receding glacier
and the terminal moraine which marked its outer reaches.
About 12,000 years ago the rising sea breached these
moraines at the Verrazano Narrows. Hudson Lake released
its waters into the present day channel of the Hudson River.
The channel had been established 120 million years earlier,
when the continents split apart and the Palisades were
exposed. The East River, actually a tidal straight connecting
the Long Island Sound and the New York Harbor, was formed
11,000 years ago at the end of the Wisconsin glaciations. As
the sea continued to rise, reaching its modern level about
6,000 years ago the archipelago of New York City emerged.

The discovery of a glacial erratic buried on the Edge site
in Williamsburg by the contractors digging a foundation
for the building was thus an event to be celebrated. An
erratic is a rock carried from some other location often
hundreds of miles away and dropped as the glacier melted
in a place with different bedrock. This rock was the size
of a Volkswagen and had probably been brought from the
Palisades, or maybe Canada, before it was dropped as the
glacier receded. Having survived the grinding of the glacier,
its normal reward for this journey would be to be smashed
up and hauled off as gravel. When we found out about this
discovery, we immediately petitioned the owner to save it
and make it a part of the landscape. Exposing evidence of
this slow migration of frozen water and debris 11,000 years
ago is a counterpoint to the present flux of tides, ferries, and
people to the site. The rock now rests intact at the terminus
of N. 5th Street, welcoming newcomers to the park.

GATEWAY: (UN)NATURAL SELECTION

National Parks have historically been about preserving and protecting a place of scenic beauty—removed and ideally "untouched" by humans. Gateway is different. A park along the edge of one of the largest cities in the world, that passes by one of the busiest airports in the world and is itself a historical artifact in the history of flight, cannot exist as ,or pretend to be, "untouched"; it has to be something different.

Our design celebrates the process of (un)natural selection. In the 21st century, we're beginning to understand that human health and ecology exist within, and not separate from, the surrounding environment. At Gateway, our design emphasizes the give and take of this relationship, and the ways that natural ecologies have been shaped by humans directly and indirectly.

Gateway is situated in the critical area between the barrier islands and the mainland. The unique and complex site has been formed by the movements of the larger Hudson River estuary and by its ocean edge condition. We re-orient the visitor experience to the water as the unifier of this diverse landscape, creating a continuous waterfront pathway and a ferry system to link the sites. Many of the sites with cultural significance, especially Floyd Bennet Field, are adjacent to or overlap with sites of potential ecological importance to the community and the region, but which have become severely altered and degraded through human use. Our design re-establishes a water based ecology and heightens the proximity of the ecological and the cultural, giving new uses to the existing structures, which emphasize the interwoven-ness of this shared landscape while distinguishing the differences and specificity of each nook.

Our design strategy involves three overlapping steps: re-orient the experience of the visitor from the fragment to the whole, restore elements that have been lost or severely degraded, and preserve those remaining elements that have cultural or ecological value.

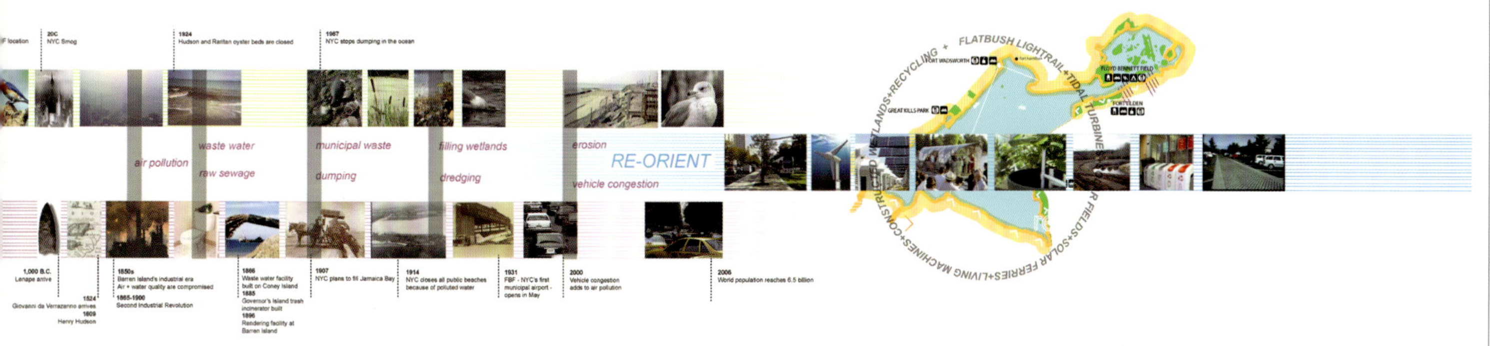

1   Timeline of cultural and ecological events merging with our plan

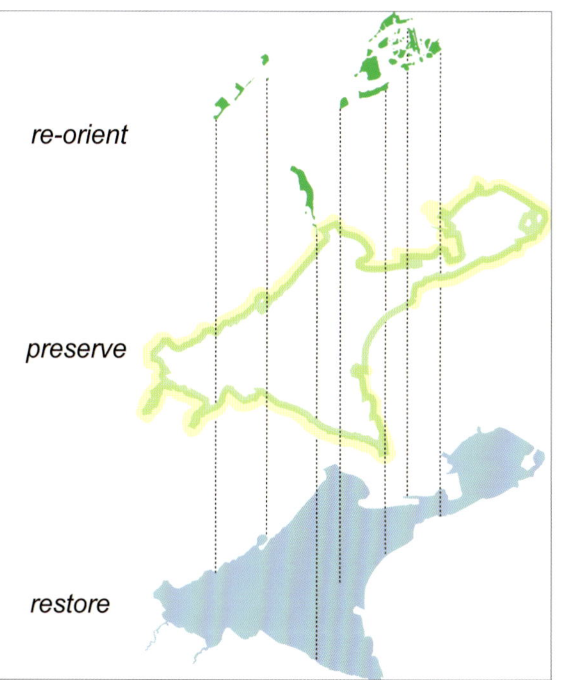

2   Three part strategy for change

3   Rendering of runway next to newly created wetland

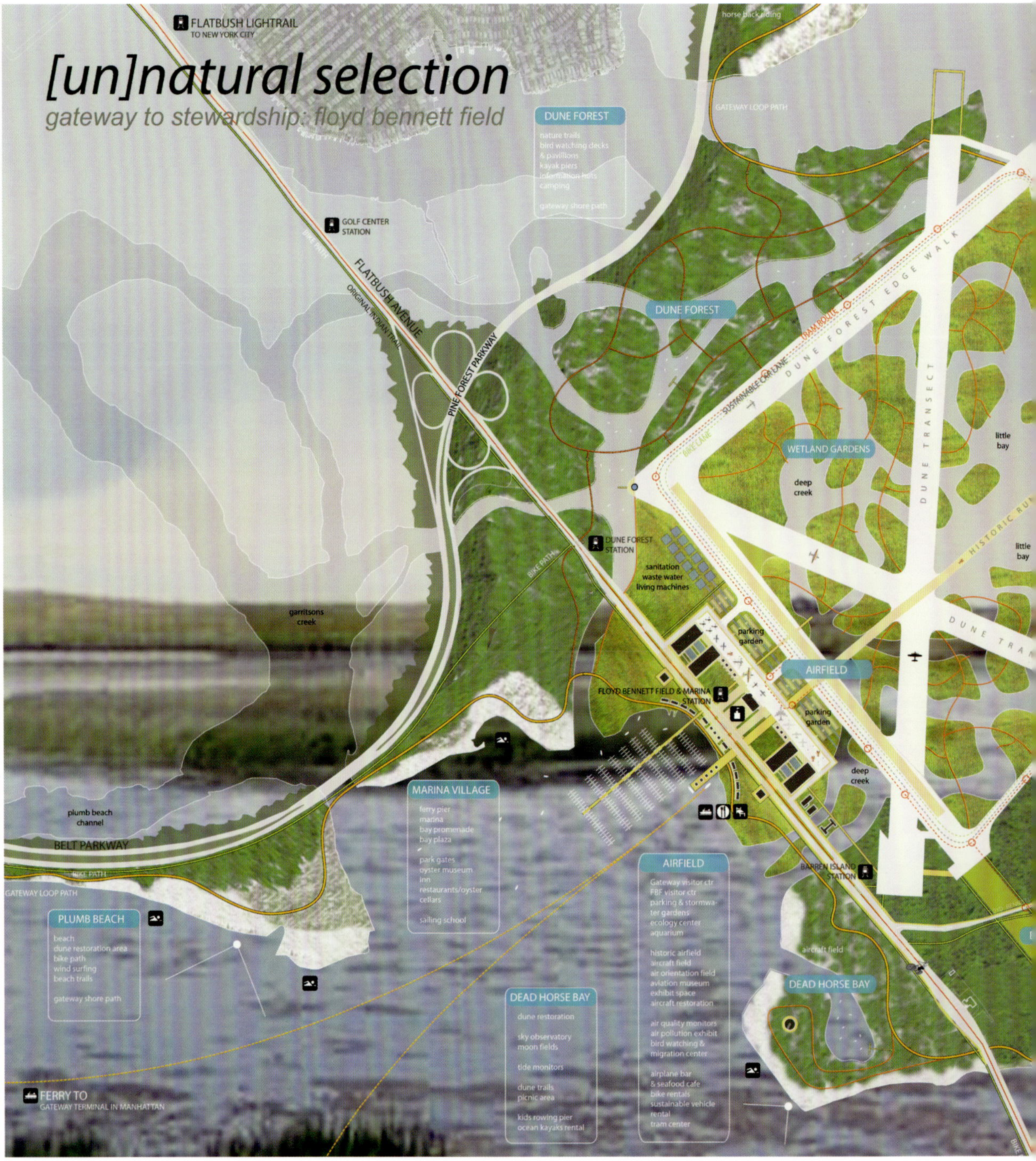

[un]natural selection
gateway to stewardship: floyd bennett field

4   Plan of a reimagined Floyd Bennett Field, where wetlands merge with history
and new uses on one of our winning competition boards

Envisioning Gateway

Envisioning Gateway was a public design competition held in 2007 to re-envision Gateway- the first urban National Recreation Area. Designated in 1972, exactly one century after Yellowstone became the first national park in the United States and the world, it struggles to meet the aspirations of its founders. Thirty-five years later, the partnership of Van Alen Institute, National Parks Conservation Association, and Columbia University Graduate School of Architecture Planning and Preservation invited designers worldwide to play a vital role in Gateway National Recreation Area's future by generating innovative, visionary, and compelling proposals that celebrate the unique potential of the park as both a significant regional resource and a national environmental treasure. We were among the six award winners of the competition, and are featured in the subsequent publication "Gateway: Voices for an Urban National Park" by Princeton Architectural Press, 2011.

5   Existing Floyd Bennett Field

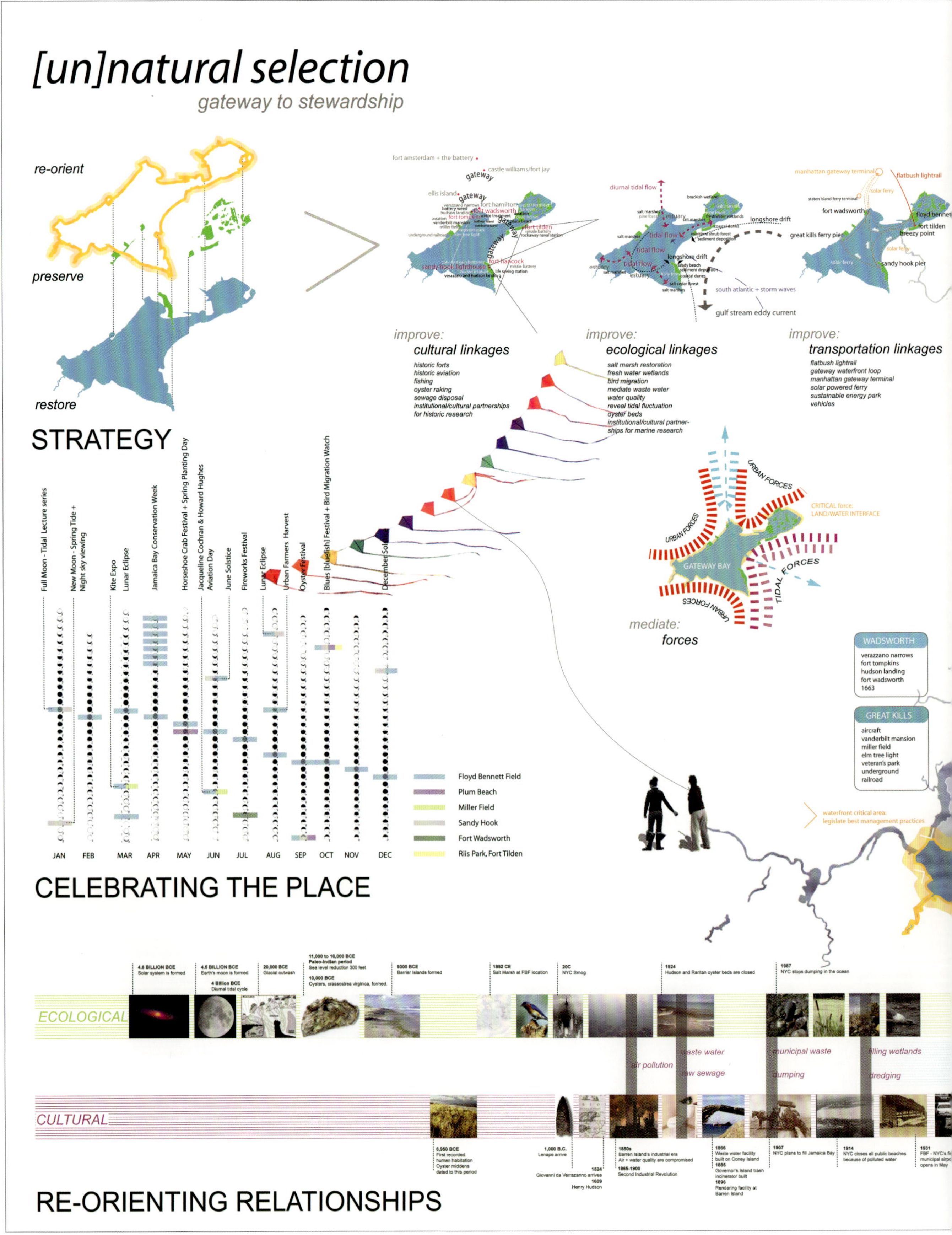
[un]natural selection
gateway to stewardship

re-orient
preserve
restore

STRATEGY

improve:
cultural linkages
historic forts
historic aviation
fishing
oyster raking
sewage disposal
institutional/cultural partnerships
for historic research

improve:
ecological linkages
salt marsh restoration
fresh water wetlands
bird migration
mediate waste water
water quality
reveal tidal fluctuation
oyster beds
institutional/cultural partnerships for marine research

improve:
transportation linkages
flatbush lightrail
gateway waterfront loop
manhattan gateway terminal
solar powered ferry
sustainable energy park
vehicles

mediate:
forces

URBAN FORCES
TIDAL FORCES
GATEWAY BAY
CRITICAL force:
LAND/WATER INTERFACE

WADSWORTH
verazzano narrows
fort tompkins
hudson landing
fort wadsworth
1663

GREAT KILLS
aircraft
vanderbilt mansion
miller field
elm tree light
veteran's park
underground
railroad

CELEBRATING THE PLACE

Full Moon - Tidal Lecture series
New Moon - Spring Tide + Night sky viewing
Kite Expo
Lunar Eclipse
Jamaica Bay Conservation Week
Horseshoe Crab Festival + Spring Planting Day
Jacqueline Cochran & Howard Hughes Aviation Day
June Solstice
Fireworks Festival
Lunar Eclipse
Urban Farmers Harvest
Oyster Festival
Blues [bluefish] Festival + Bird Migration Watch
December Sol

JAN FEB MAR APR MAY JUN JUL AUG SEP OCT NOV DEC

Floyd Bennett Field
Plum Beach
Miller Field
Sandy Hook
Fort Wadsworth
Riis Park, Fort Tilden

ECOLOGICAL
CULTURAL

RE-ORIENTING RELATIONSHIPS

1943—twelve Russian scientist starve to death rather than eat seeds
in Pavlousk seed bank during siege of Leningrad

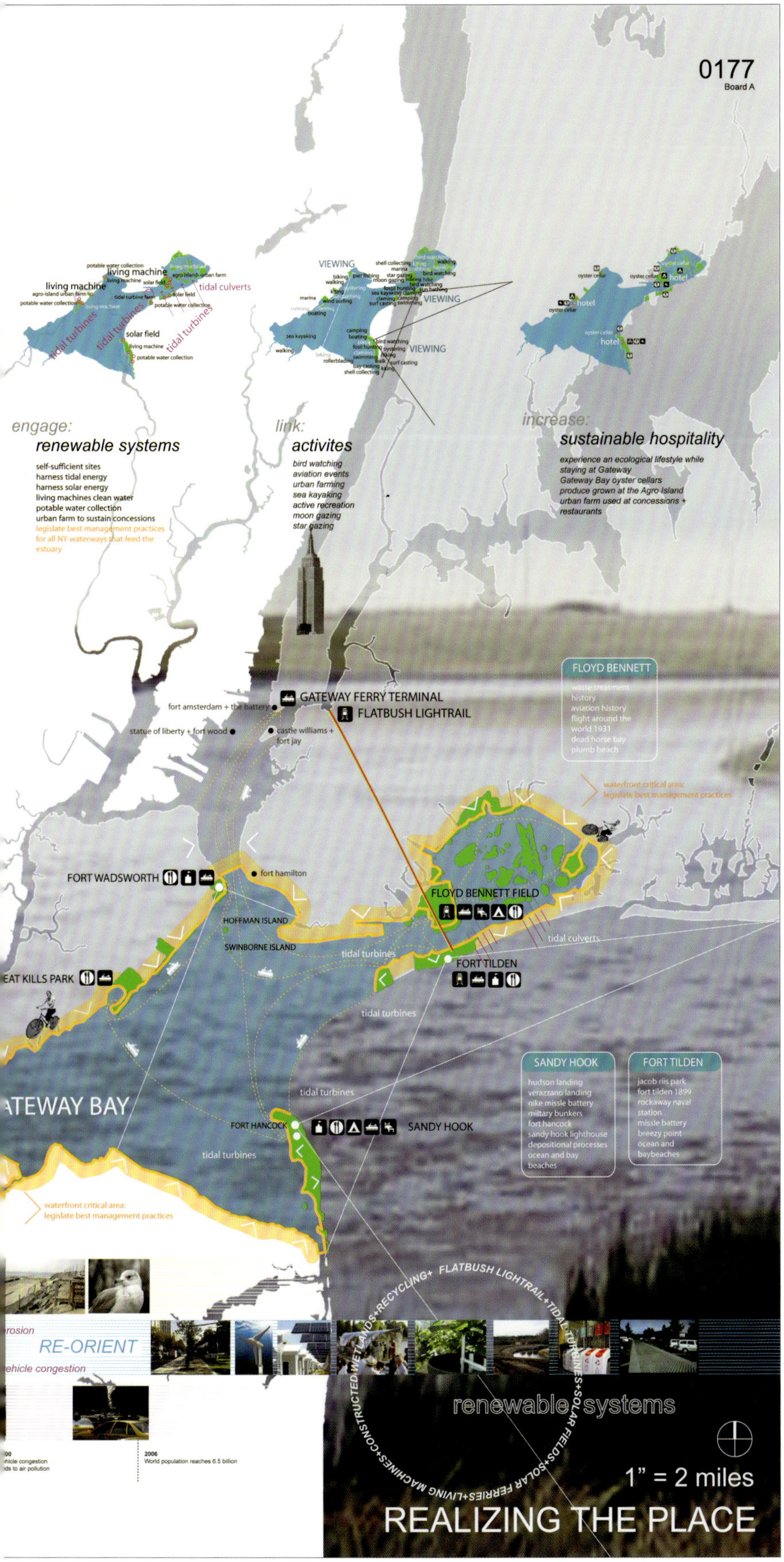

0177
Board A

engage:
renewable systems

self-sufficient sites
harness tidal energy
harness solar energy
living machines clean water
potable water collection
urban farm to sustain concessions
legislate best management practices
for all NY waterways that feed the
estuary

link:
activites

bird watching
aviation events
urban farming
sea kayaking
active recreation
moon gazing
star gazing

increase:
sustainable hospitality

experience an ecological lifestyle while
staying at Gateway
Gateway Bay oyster cellars
produce grown at the Agro Island
urban farm used at concessions +
restaurants

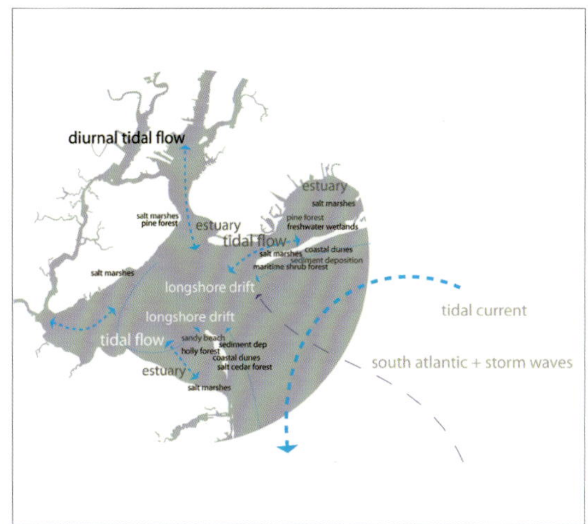

7   Using the Tidal flows in the Bay

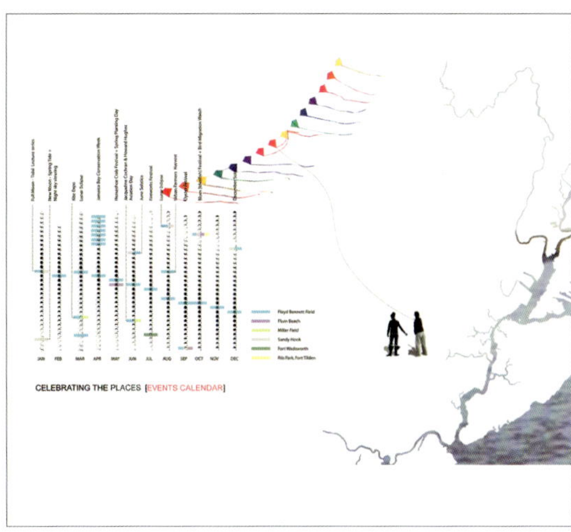

8   Calendar of events to celebrate the place

REBUILD BY DESIGN

Coastal Commercial Resiliency

Rebuild by Design is a multi-stage regional design competition funded by the U.S. Department of Housing and Urban Development (HUD) and launched by the President's Hurricane Sandy Rebuilding Task Force. Ten teams were chosen to participate in the research and collaborative analysis of the Sandy-affected region to identify key design opportunities.

Our team, lead by HR&A with Cooper Robertson, focused on the resiliency challenges of commercial corridors across the region. During the research phase, we organized possible sites into three categories based on land typology: barrier island, mainland coastal, and dense urban edge. This provided a framework for thinking about the ecological, built, and economic conditions associated with each typology and how they could move toward resiliency.

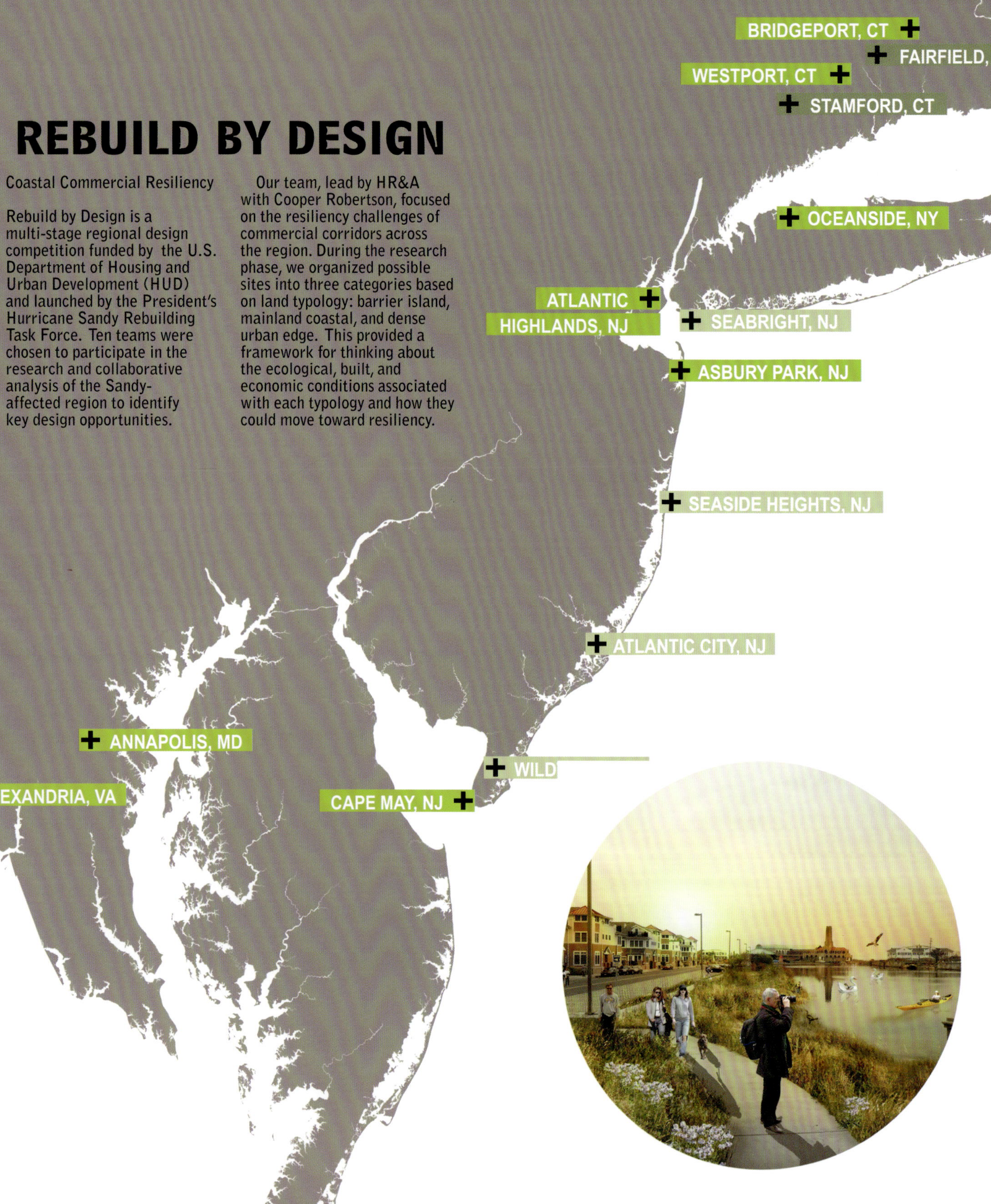

Ecological

| barrier island | mainland coastal | dense urban edge |

 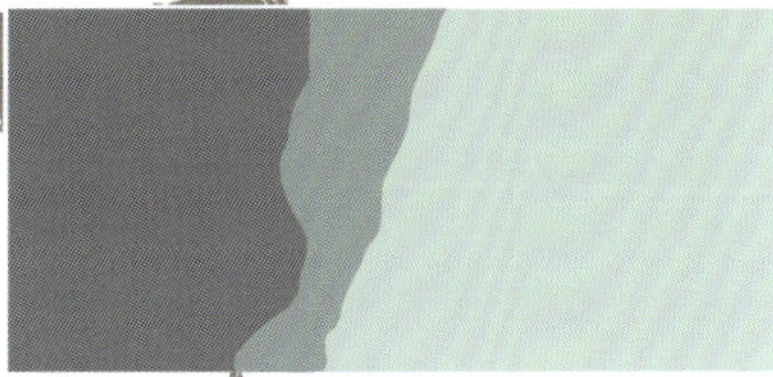  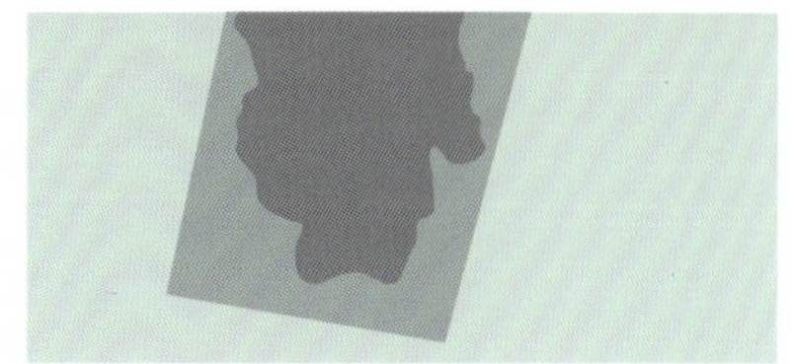

barrier island	mainland coastal	dense urban edge
Completely in flood plain	Dune system on ocean side	Artificial edge bounds dense urban fabric
Wetland system on bay side	Flooding from one edge	High amounts of impervious cover
Dune system on ocean side		Storm sewer drainage issues
Wave action on ocean side		

Built

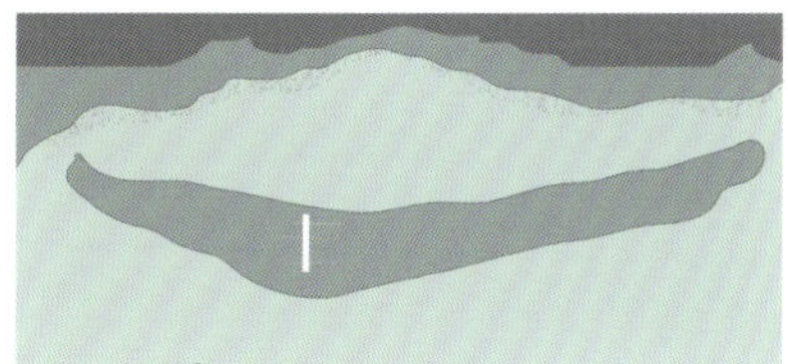 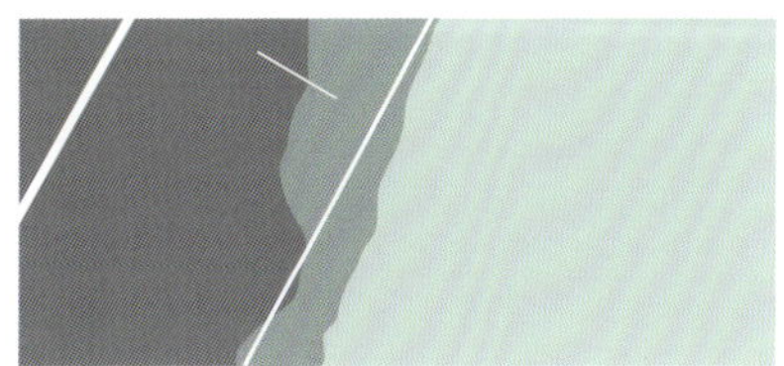 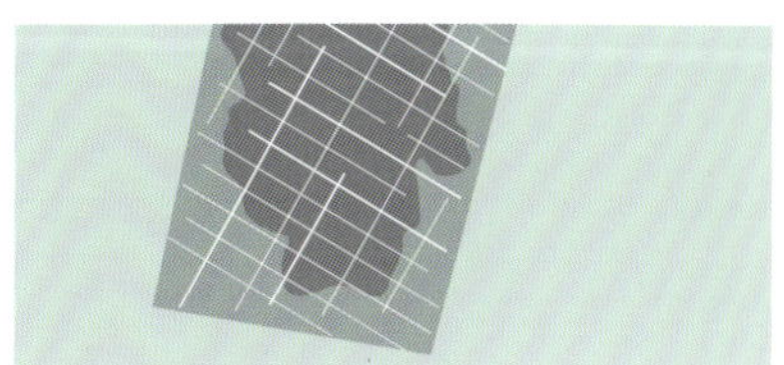

barrier island	mainland coastal	dense urban edge
Parallel commercial corridor has one sided retail	Main street retail is primarily vehicular and on higher ground	Dense network of commercial corridors extend into flood plain
Perpendicular corridor has two sided retail | natural boundaries	Pedestrian retail stretches between main street and boardwalk	High density provides limited opportunity for retreat

Economic

barrier island	mainland coastal	dense urban edge
Highly seasonal economy	Depends on seasonal tourism and local consumers	Supported by urban consumers and tourism
Lower density population	Low to moderate sales per capita	Varied levels of retail sales per capita
Provides seasonal jobs to local low to mid - income residents	Provides jobs for local low to mid- income residents	Provides jobs for low to mid income residents

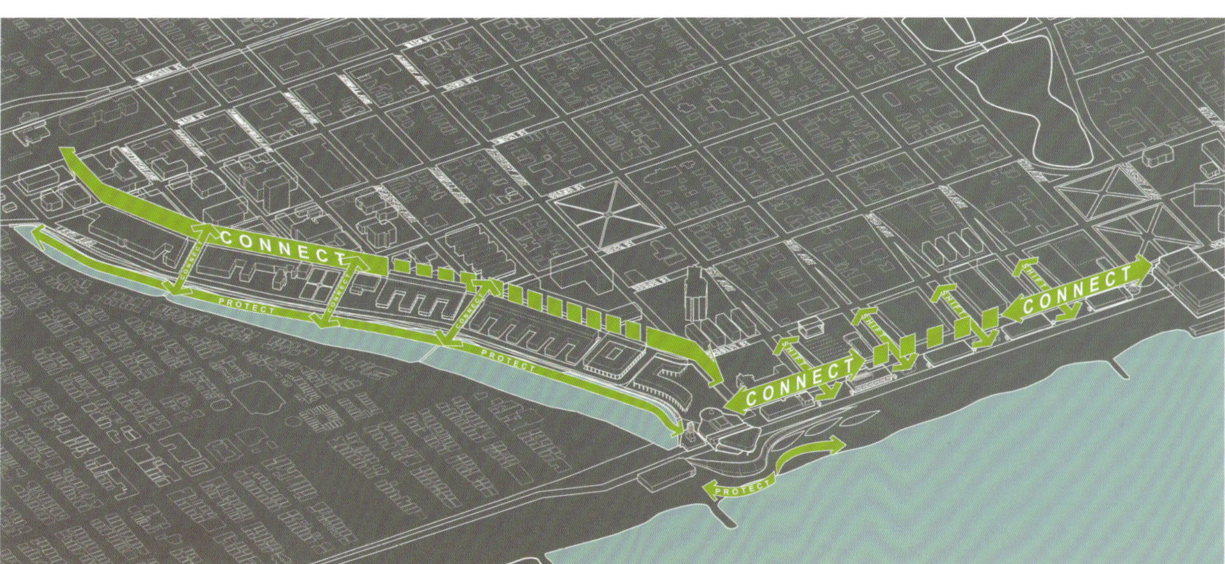

GLIMPSES 2040

Dredgescape: An Estuary Evolution

NYC is a marine city built on the world's fourth largest estuary. Since its founding in the early 1600s until the late 1900's, this environment has been in decline and its great biodiversity has been replaced by cultural diversity. This proposal creates a new infrastructure for uniting these disparate realms. As more and more NYC coastline is converted from industrial to recreational uses, this proposal seeks sustainable relationships of exchange between working and recreational waterfronts, terrestrial, and aquatic habitats.

The Estuary Edge

In the 1600s, it is estimated that over 1000 acres of salt marsh enhanced the shores of Manhattan Island. Today there is less than 100. Salt marsh and other tidal wetland habitat play a vital role in the stability of the environment. Wetlands retain and gradually release large quantities of water which otherwise would flow more quickly out to sea. Their dense vegetation traps sediments and consumes pollutants. Above water, the plant material takes in large amounts of carbon dioxide and releases great quantities of oxygen, much the way rain forests do. With their large food supplies, they also encourage and sustain a multitude of species.

The Port

NYC is the third largest port in the US. Plans for the port include continued dredging to keep it operational and to deepen it to allow passage by the larger "Post-Panamax" vessels. This dredging allows for more material to be sent by water, the most efficient means of transport, especially when it is connected to rails to send it further inland. This in turn keeps trucks off of the roads, improving air quality. Water quality is improving in the estuary due to cleaner industries mandated by the Clean Water Act, making the water and waterfront appealing venues for recreation after decades of industrial use contaminated and dominated them.

Recreation—Launchings and Landings and Marine Streets

The wide Hudson currently has very few places of refuge for boaters from sudden changes in the weather or wakes of large ships. For the river to attract human powered craft operated by a wide range of skill levels, more places of refuge are needed that will also link amenities. Animals also require habitat that has been reduced over the centuries as wetlands have been filled. Using the dredge material that is currently shipped south, we propose to create new "archipelagos" to create a system of places for refuge and exploration along the Hudson estuary. This system will include both launches and landings, allowing for increased water access by human powered crafts and for large and small loops to be navigated by boaters of all ages and skill levels. Dredge material from the shipping channel will be recycled every year to create archipelagos further and further upstream. By 2040, travelers will be able to adventure along and across the Hudson for day trips or overnights— from Jamaica Bay north to Troy—engaging with the river on journeys that erase the boundaries between wilderness recreation and urban travel.

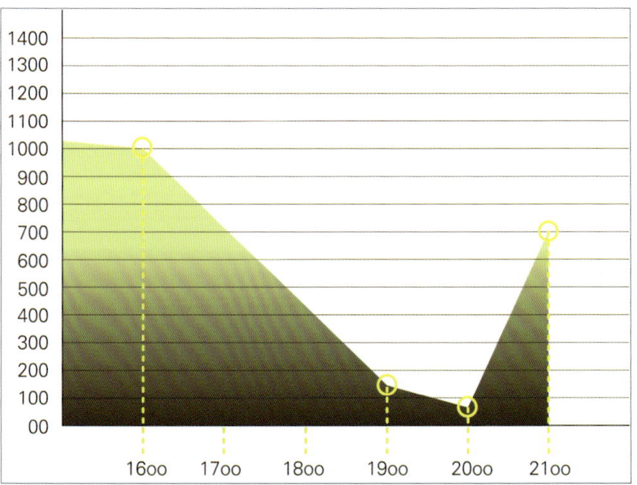

1 Declining acres of wetlands in the NYC area and projected increase due to this project

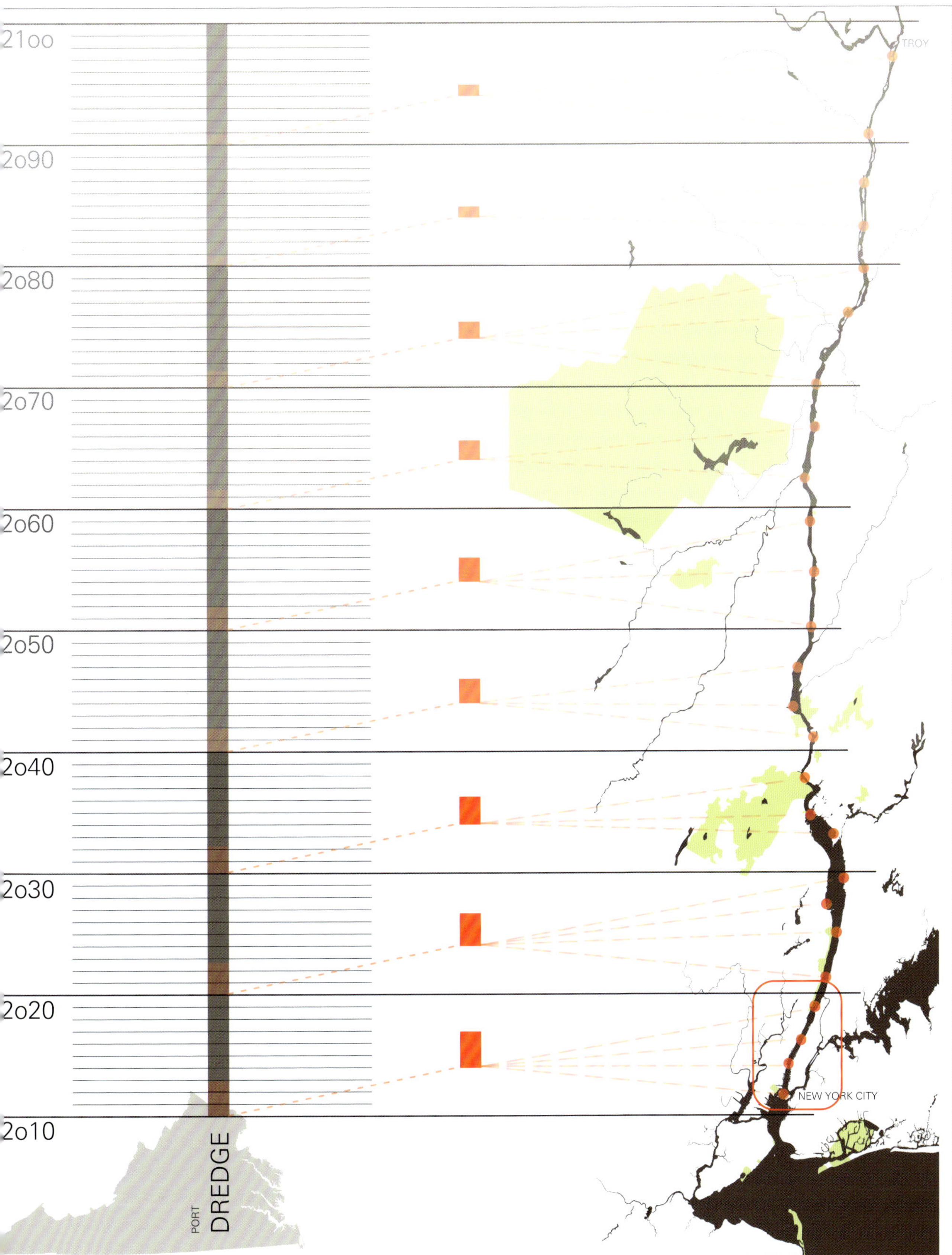

2   Percentage of dredge reused to create the archipelago of islands up the Hudson

3   dredging is a constant in the NYC harbor

Beginning in Manhattan and across the river in Hoboken and Weehawken, our first three archipelagos will allow for better connection across this wide river. As Hudson Yards and the High Line engage the Hudson River Park, this new marine edge, the archipelagos, and Marine Streets, will provide access into the water itself. By 2040, we will create a new infrastructure for human or wind powered craft to explore the Hudson, and for wading, fishing, and boating from the Battery to Troy.

Access

This system of island archipelagos will connect to the city through 'Marine Streets'— places in the city grid where the urban landscape breaks and eases into a more wild one, providing direct access to the water. Marine streets mitigate the boundaries between the water and the land, creating a system of interchange between the urban and the wild, and in doing so create an expanded infrastructure for filtering and slowing water inflows and outflows between the river and city—protecting the city from sudden surges in the water level, and the water from the runoff of the city streets.

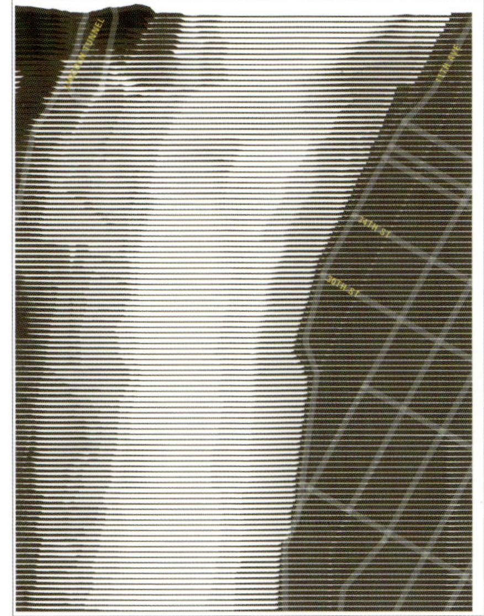

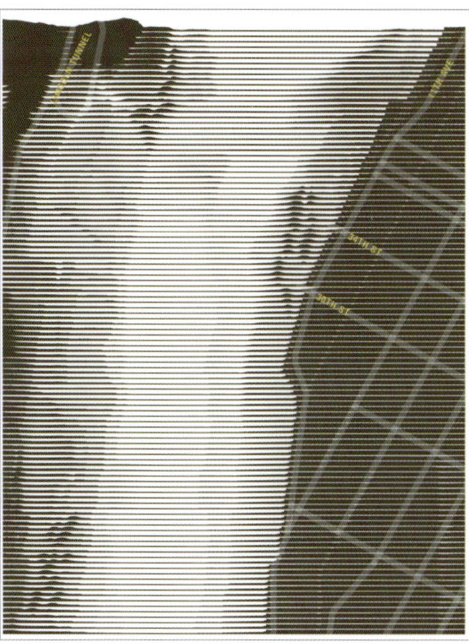

4   Hudson River at 42nd st existing

5   Hudson River at 42nd St proposed with island archipelagos

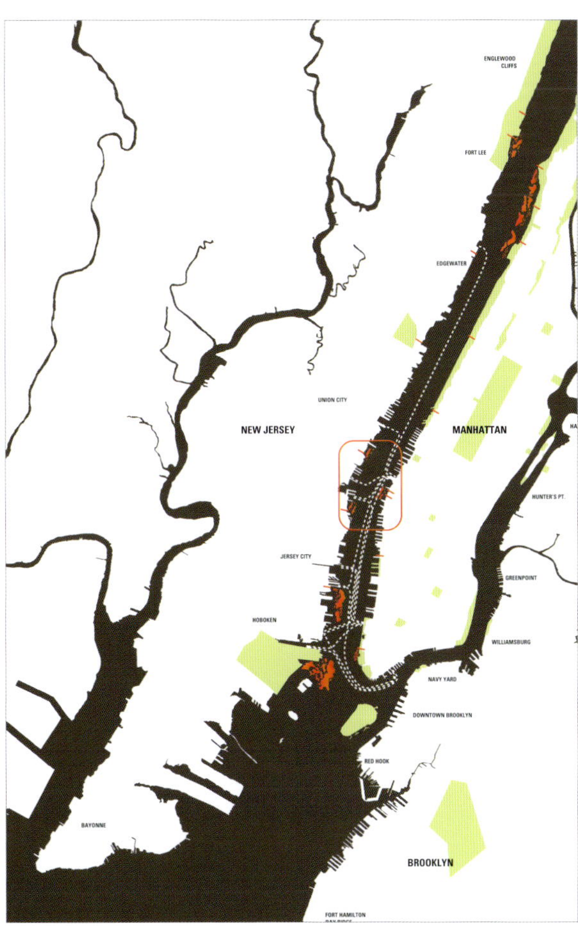

9   Archipelago island groupings in the Hudson located at intervals to provide safe harbors for small craft

7   Breathing—The I J River—by our Amsterdam partner,
Delva Landscape Architects and Dingeman Diys Architect

Breathing—Uniting bio
and cultural diversity

We seek to create sustainable
relationships of exchange
between the working and
recreational waterfronts as
well as creating terrestrial
and aquatic habitat for a wide
species of animals. The iconic
landscape of the Hudson River
School will be reimagined
as a new iconic landscape
celebrating the reunification
of the cultural and the natural
in a sustainable future.

Glimpses 2040—New
York /Amsterdam was
an invited exhibition
at the Center for
Architecture in
2011. As an exchange
program between
the Center and the
Amsterdam Center for
Architecture (ARCAM)
the organizations
commissioned five
teams from New York
and five teams from
Amsterdam to look
at five different
aspects of their
cities: breathing,
eating, dwelling,
making, and moving
and to contemplate
"the future of the
future". We were
assigned "breathing".

10   Island dredgescape for
boating, exploration, habitat, water
quality improvements, as well
as storm surge mitigation.

1962—Friendship 7 mission—John Glenn first man to orbit the earth.

STRUCTURING
A LIVING
MARINE EDGE

Sloped Street end as tidal marsh.

Service Street with bioretention below parking.

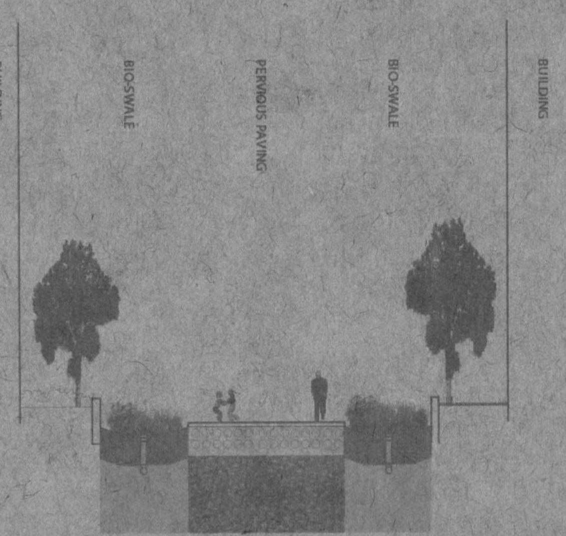

Park Street with Bio-Swales

New York City is one of the greatest marine cities of the world with 520 miles of ever-changing shoreline. The buffering functions of wetlands and dynamic ecological communities which have historically filtered runoff and protected the land from storms have been gradually erased. With increased urbanization, our once rich and dynamic shoreline is often reduced to a single line of bulkhead. In addition, increased runoff from development, and upland impermeable surfaces, contribute to flooding and sewer overflows in the New York City area on a regular basis.

As New York City continues to promote development on the waterfront (NYC DCP, 2011), existing underutilized street ends have the potential to provide better connection to the waterfront with enormous ecological and social gain. Just as the MilliontreesNYC initiative (NYC DPR, 2011) has a great public and ecological value, a "Marine Streets" initiative would help sustain the living resource of the rivers and bays. We envision these "Marine Streets" as a new street typology; a critical edge which would mitigate both the upland urban runoff and the climatic tidal surges while providing residents with an improved sense of place and a heightened awareness of their great marine city. Functioning ecologically-based on the dynamics of the natural wetlands, they would remain accessible for human use with careful planning and design. These improvements could be made now, concurrent with, or prior to, planned upland development, providing a means to improve the environment within the existing redevelopment framework of streets and blocks.

Dead end streets exist in all five boroughs on approximately 25% of the shoreline. Most are underutilized, and support little traffic, either vehicular or pedestrian. The street is often in poor physical condition, and the edge where land and water meet is a barrier, often fenced, prohibiting access to the water's edge. Changing these poorly used streets to Marine Streets would provide an infrastructure that enhances ecological conditions and provides a strong social interaction between the people of the city and their river.

The ecological function is two fold: it will address storm water runoff from the upland as well as storm surges and rising tides from the water side. From the uplands, New York City currently spills 520 gallons of sewage into waterways per week on average, according to Riverkeeper, a local advocacy group. Because sewage and storm water are collected in the same pipes, sewage floods directly into rivers when the system is overwhelmed by storms. The basic idea for Marine Streets is to remove the asphalt street surface and replace it with a permeable surface which allows the landscape and soils to move, store, and filter rainwater, slowing runoff into the rivers and storm systems. This would help improve water quality by slowing the quantity of runoff into the combined system, reducing the amount of sewage let into the rivers. The quality of the water reaching the river can also be improved by filtering the water through various types of vegetated filters, (bioswales, filter strips, raingardens, etc) which reduce, minimize or remove, depending on the particular design of the filter, suspended solids and heavy metals(30-90%), nutrients such as phosphorous or nitrogen (10-65%) and oils and grease.(City of Chicago, BMP)

From the water side the new sloped marine streets would help mitigate some of the effects of proposed climate change. With climate change, an increased sea level rise of approximately 58 cm (2 feet) and perhaps as much as 116 cm (4 feet) is anticipated in the next hundred years (NYC DCP, 2011). Marine Streets are designed to slope gradually from the lower tidal elevations up to the street above hundred year flood level. When properly designed, the depressed street will encourage growth of the rich intertidal environment and estuarine habitats , much like the natural salt marshes and wetlands that used to be prevalent here. Storm surges and powerful storm currents would be buffered and partially absorbed by the vegetated slopes of the former street. This area also provides habitat for terrestrial as well as aquatic species, increasing local biodiversity.

The streets would remain accessible for pedestrian use, providing social as well as ecological benefits. The perception of being a part of a great marine city will be enhanced by the presence of the water now as much as 1500 feet further inland in the underutilized streetbed. The daily tidal changes would become more a part of the life of the city, as would seasonal differences in river edge ecology.

With careful planning and design, varying amounts of vehicular access can be accommodated if desired or needed. Occasional use by service vehicles or vehicular access only partially down the length of the street are possible variations. Three basic street types would allow for various mixes of pedestrian and vehicular use to serve adjacent uses and allow as much of the street as possible to be put to multiple uses, creating an new ecology of the edge which embraces both environmental and human needs.

New York City is behind in recognizing the singular importance of this marine edge. The Maryland General Assembly passed the Chesapeake Bay Critical Areas legislation in 1984 to protect and control runoff in the edge areas of this important estuary (Critical Areas Commission, 2011). The Critical Area includes the Chesapeake Bay, its tributaries to the head of the tide, tidal wetlands, plus all land and water within 1000 feet beyond the landward boundary of these waters and wetlands. Instituting a Marine Streets program would establish this similar 300 meter (975 foot) stretch of public street as a unique condition worthy of special treatment and protection in the Hudson River estuary system.

This incremental approach and accretion of this ecological edge would benefit from the creation of a city wide program that would help overcome many of the existing hurdles. Maintenance agreements may require approvals by the DOT and Department of Parks and Recreation as well. And finally, if changes are required to the water's edge, to lower the bulkhead for instance, permitting is required by state and federal entities including the U. S. Army Corps of Engineers, the State Department of the Environment, etc. Coordination of these agencies through a program wide interface would also speed the approvals process.

The Marine Streets program would provide, in these ways, ecological services and a greater public amenity within current street infrastructure, where the "normal" street configuration abuts the marine zone. The ecological and social advantages of Marine Streets create a functional and appealing new city zone at this critical area, instead of the current poor meshing of street grid and the coastal zone living environment.

This proposal for Marine Streets was published in Ecological Restoration journal in September 2011. This is an abridged form.

Planting palette suggestions for Sloped Marine Streets. These native species are tolerant of salty winds and soil typical of tidally-influenced habitats.

Graminoids in the Marsh Zones

Spartina alterniflora	salt marsh cordgrass
Spartina patens	salt meadow cordgrass
Distichlis spicata	salt grass
Juncus gerardii	black rush
Scirpus pungens	common three-square sedge

Herbs in the Marsh Zones

Limonium carolinianum	sea lavender
Solidago sempervirens	seaside goldenrod
Aster tenuifolius	perennial salt marsh aster
Sabatia dodecandra	perennial sea pink
Salicornia virginica	glasswort

Woody Plants in the Marsh Zones

Baccharis halimifolia	groundsel tree
Iva frutescens	marsh elder

Trees in Upland Areas

Juniperus virginiana	eastern red cedar
Sassafras albidum	sassafras
Prunus serotina	wild cherry
Amelanchier canadensis	serviceberry

Shrubs in Upland Areas

Amorpha fruticosa	false indigo
Clethra alnifolia	sweet pepperbush
Myrica pensylvanica	northern bayberry
Prunus maritima	beach plum
Quercus ilicifolia	bear oak
Quercus prinoides	dwarf chestnut oak

Herbaceous Plants for Upland Meadows

Asclepias syriaca	common milkweed
Asclepias tuberosa	butterfly milkweed
Aster novae-angliae	New England aster
Aster novi-belgii	New York aster
Hibiscus moscheutos	swamp rose mallow
Kosteletzkya virginica	seashore mallow
Liatris scariosa	northern blazing star
Monarda fistulosa	wild bergamot

Graminoids for Upland Meadows

Panicum virgatum	switchgrass
Sorghastrum nutans	indiangrass
Schizachyrium scoparium	little bluestem

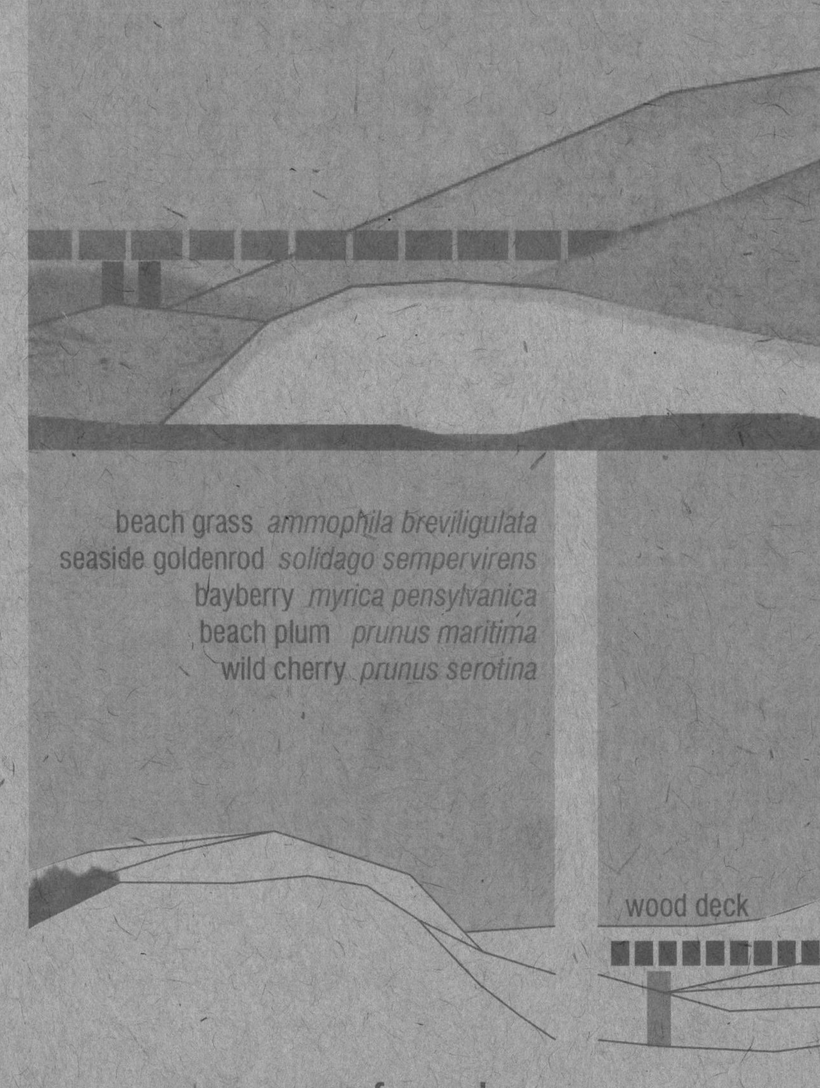

bearberry arctostaphylos uva-ursi
bech heather hudsonia tomentosa
iceland moss cetraria islandica
earth star geaster hygrometricus
trail biodome / animal watch shelter
secondary dune
oyster shell surface trail at grade

HIGH PLAINS — CALGARY

...now, the entity of a river can be established either in relation
to its name (a trace of human adventure) or to its hydrographic
entireness (the adventure of the water from its remotest head
spring down to the sea, without any record of the names given to
various segments). The problem is that the two adventures rarely
coincide. Usually the explorer's adventure goes against the stream,
starting from the sea; on the contrary the river's adventure ends
in it. The explorer who proceeds upstream has to toss his way at
each branching since above each confluence everything becomes
rarified: the water, at times the air, but always his own certainty;
whereas the river that flows down towards the sea gradually
condenses its waters and the certainty of its ineluctable way.

Annemarie Sauzeau-boetti

1   The edge of the Canadian Rockies
with the High Plains to the east

2   Downtown Calgary and the
Bow and Elbow rivers

ST PATRICK'S ISLAND

Springing from one of the world's most scenic biosystems—The Banff and Jasper National Parks in Canada—the Bow River curves through Calgary. St. Patrick's Island on the Bow is one of the city's oldest parks, but in recent years it was underutilized and perceived as dangerous. In addition, the ecological diversity had been weakened by invasive species, filling and clearing, and seeding of lawn. Our design is meant to catalyze an influx of new residents to the downtown creating a public space to link people to the processes and ecologies of the braided river.

Our design highlights the ephemeral nature of the river: allowing the landscape to change with the rising and falling of the river. Through excavation, we transformed previously disturbed areas of the site into new channels to increase engagement with the water, enhancing visitor opportunities for interaction with the water's edge. The Seasonal Breach with its rocky shores and gravel beach and the Lowland Channel wetland extend the ecologies of the island to allow a full spectrum of diversity for visitors to explore and discover.

These changes and excavations left behind an excess of excavated soil. Using this waste, we created a Rise in a previously cleared area at the center of the island. The Rise creates a visual connection between the island and the city, a place to look back at the City from the surrounding natural reserve. The Rise also delivers a note of man-made fantasy on an island where many spaces highlight the ecological processes that would take place without the interference of humans.

Where the island is physically linked to the mainland and an adjacent island, we created a new gateway to the island experience—the Lookout. Here, more heavily programmed activities are grouped together creating a place to gather and orient, to begin the journey out to the more natural areas of the island.

In keeping with the ecological mission of the park, we also set aside parts of the island to regenerate with little disturbance from visitors. The central part of the Gallery Forest will be closed to park activity, allowing the island ecology to mature and rebuild its rich mosaic of plant and animal communities.

1 Group of existing mature poplars in the fall

2   Competition drawing of entry plaza below the Lookout
Pavilion looking out towards the new wetland

a

b

c

a   Proposed Seasonal Breech

b   Existing lawn area at proposed seasonal breech

c   Proposed seasonal breech n winter

d   View of St Patricks Island (in foreground)

3   Plan of the proposed St Patrick's Island Park

d

4   Detail plan of the Seasonal Breech

a   Early sketch by Barbara

b   Early sketch by Mark

c   Alternative sketch by Mark

c

Collaboration Mark Johnson
The scale of the western landscape, especially in Canada, is huge. Complex relationships between land forms and their formative processes give rise to plant communities and various ecologies. Mark Johnson understands the West—how it was formed, and how those processes have shaped each place, why the plants grow where they do, where the water is. As most of our projects to date in North America had been on the East Coast, we wanted a firm with an understanding of the West to work with us in Calgary. Denver, the home of Civitas's offices, is the US high plains equivalent of Calgary.

As Mark is a landscape architect, you cannot point to a singular place of his influence, but rather it is felt throughout. He challenged us with his language, he challenged us with his drawings, and he challenged us with his field observations. We had a lively exchange through all phases of the project, but especially at the beginning, where the concepts of the land formation, the patterns of erosion and deposition in this braided section of the river, shaped the new island forms. He also is a great story teller, and as a result was a hit with the media—able to clearly explain what we were doing and why. Walking a landscape with Mark is a learning experience in observation and analysis, leading from the head, but with laughter and stories from the heart.

Project Team

Client:
Calgary Municipal
Land Corporation

Landscape Architect:
W/Civitas

Architect:
W Architecture and
Landscape Architecture

Landscape Architect and
Architect of Record:
IBI Group

Structural Engineer:
Guy Nordenson Engineers

Structural Engineer
of Record:
Read Jones Christofferson

Electrical Engineer:
SMP

Lighting Designer:
TIllet Lighting

Mechanical Engineer:
SNC Lavalin

Civil Engineer
IBI Group

Hydrology:
Matrix Solutions, Inc

Cost Estimator:
BTY

Signage Designers:
J Communications

Bench Designers:
JPI-Jeremy Pavka
Industries

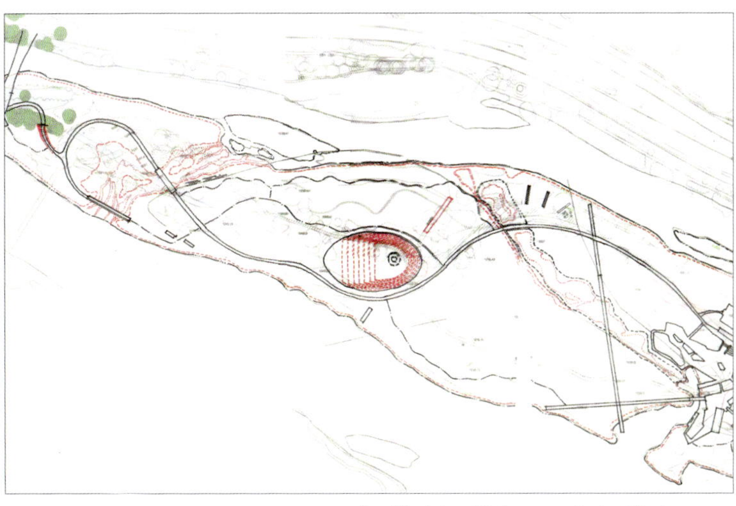

5   Sketch with topography by Mark

Collaboration Guy Nordenson
The Lookout Pavilion at St Patrick's Island is the gateway to the park from the east and also a place to view the confluence of the Bow and Elbow Rivers. As islands are places of deposition, the idea of using small pieces of wood to work together to span a much larger area was an initial reference to similar "pile ups" of wood on the shore. Wood is also a plentiful resource in the mountains, with many glum lam providers located in the Canadian West. Guy Nordenson and Associates developed the reciprocal structure which comprises the roof of the Pavilion.

A reciprocal frame is a class of self-supporting structure made of three or more beams and which requires no center support to create roofs, bridges or similar structures. This use of load bearing elements to create a spatial configuration of mutual support has been known since antiquity. Nordenson oriented the grid of the overlap to point to the winter and summer solstice in Calgary. Thus, the Lookout not only focuses on the water, but the celestial events which define the site experience.

6   Lookout Pavilion

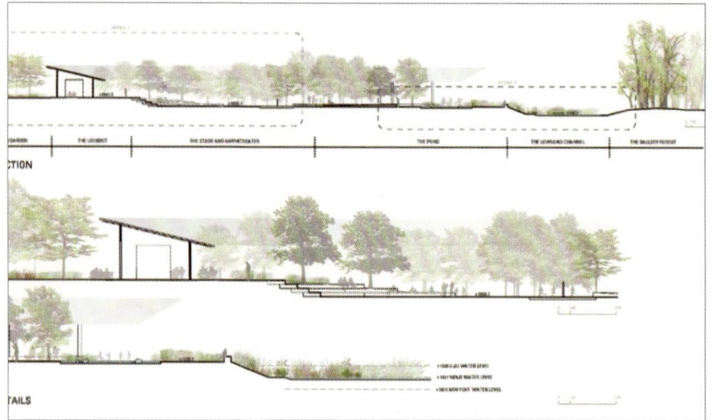

a

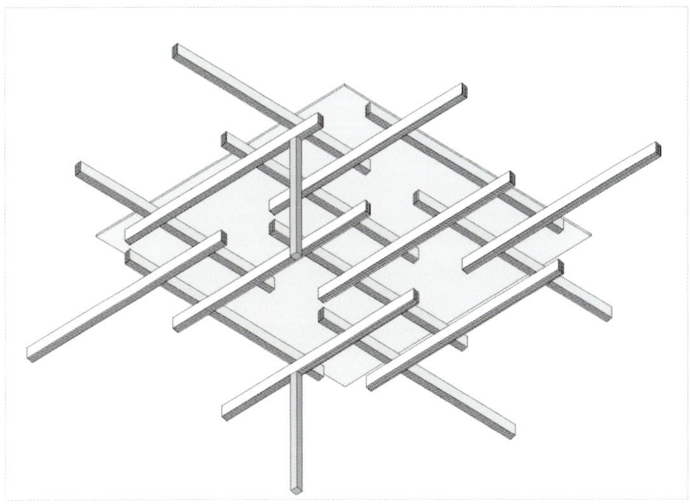

7   Axon of reciprocal structure

a   Competition sections
through Lookout Pavilion

b   Reciprocal structure studies

c   Reciprocal structure studies

b

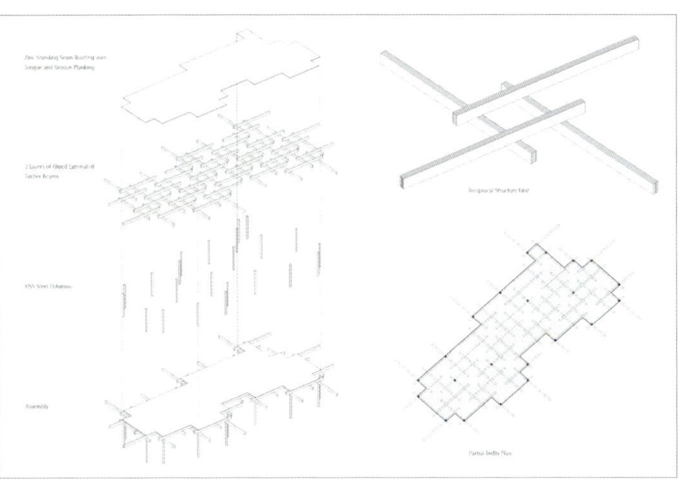

c

a

The form of the maintenance and washroom building at St Patrick's Island reflects the site location on an island in a flood plain. Sited on the highest ground on the island, it is formed as if shaped by water, positioned in the direction of the flow. It also subtly modulates the pathway, providing a gathering place in its fold, as well as a place to orient and learn about the site.

The cladding of the building is made from salvaged decking of the old pedestrian bridge that was demolished as the new bridge was constructed at the west end of the island.

b

c

d

1   View walking towards building from the east

a   Building axonometric

b   North Elevation

c   South elevation

d   Reused wood milled three ways

e   East & west elevations

f   Model views

f

8   Jon Swann leading a group looking for insects

BioBlitz—Scientists take over St Patrick's Island

Urban ecologies are hybrid systems involving the interplay of human, animal and plant communities, including temporary and permanent inhabitants. Can design interventions improve the island ecology?

On May 24 and 25, 2013 scientists from the University of Calgary and Mount Royal University as well as experts from the Calgary Field Naturalists' Society attended a 24 hour research program to itemize the living species on St Patrick's Island—a "BioBlitz". The object of this living "treasure hunt" is to find and identify plants, mammals, birds, insects, and everything else that calls the island home to create a biodiversity baseline for the island. In five years time, after our park implementation is complete, another assessment will be performed to see if the biodiversity is increasing as intended.

A temporary laboratory camp, equipped with charts, microscopes, live traps, nest boxes and white boards was set up on St Patrick's Island to allow scientific teams the opportunity to track and report their findings in support of the catalog process.

At the end of the 24 hour period, over 450 species in total were found—including birds, insects, mammals, and plants by the over 30 scientists and the many interested citizens. Construction started the next day on the new island plan.

Collaboration Steven Handel

The BioBlitz was organized by our enthusiastic ecologist, Steven Handel, who also assisted us in the plans for re-establishment of the wetland and breach ecologies. Steven goes beyond the role of scientist—educating the public about the importance of urban ecology is his passion and his enthusiasm is infectious. While many of his ideas, including a real time underwater camera and video display, did not make it into the final budget, his skill in helping us create lasting diverse environments here will be his legacy.

b

d

c

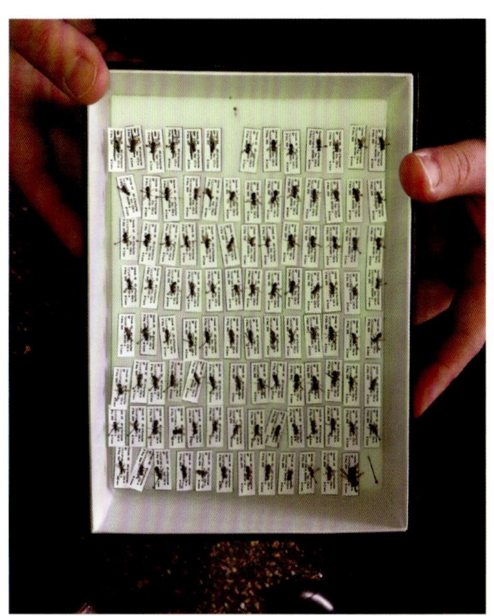

a   Box of bees

a   Box of bees

b   Looking for water creatures

c   Steven Handel and friends

d   Juvenile great horned owl

STRUCTURING FORESTS FOR A LIVING PLANET

Trees and their assemblage into diverse plant matrices or forests are a critical part of our global ecosystem. They perform works for us - from water management to air filtering to providing food and energy conversion for the planet. They offer habitat for many animal species including necessary shade for humans. They register the seasons as they adapt to the changes in light and temperature. Yet they are a scarce resource in many areas of the city as well as a dwindling habitat globally, due in part to a lack of recognition of their full benefits.

There are more than 400,000 brownfield sites in North America. Many of our projects are on these former industrial sites. Most vegetation has been erased—the soils are often fill, imported from elsewhere, sometimes contaminated. In contrast, a healthy forest is typically the result of centuries of development in particular climatic, soil, and hydrological conditions. How do you create a sustainable woodland structure in these disturbed locations?

We often start by looking back to what would have grown there pre-industry. But conditions are often so changed in the regional and local ecosystems that these plants are no longer the most viable candidates. Pests and diseases previously unknown to the region or killed off by colder winters now damage the plants and can possibly infest the broader territory. We must choose tree varieties that work best on the site as we amend it. Often these are trees that survive in flood plains or other areas where oxygen is scarce, as it is in compacted city streets.

At West Harlem Piers Park, the historic ecosystem would likely have been a Maple Swamp. However, maples can no longer be planted in New York City because of the infestation of Asian Longhorn Beetle and the Anthracnose fungus. Other natives, like the Black Tupelo and the Sassafras, are beautiful and resilient trees but are difficult to propagate or unpopular, making them unavailable commercially.

The final mix of trees to create our Harlem woodland is a diverse group ranging from native species to hearty exotics from similar climates. It is composed of 110 trees from Persia and Japan, as well as native oaks and flowering understory trees from the US. We chose these species because we thought them suited to both the urban and brackish riverside conditions. This range of scales, forms and textures will progressively develop into a diverse woodland, whose canopy will shade the site and celebrate the seasons. We will learn from monitoring their progress over time if our woodland meets our hopes.

At other sites, questions of vegetation and woodland structure are more a cultural than ecological issue. At Cornell

University for instance, where our project straddled the edge
of the campus overlooking the steep slopes of the gorge, two
landscape systems exist. A manicured quadrangle landscape
of lawn and trees (mostly Elms planted before Dutch Elm
disease) is situated next to the steep gorge edges and the
largely untended "native" vegetation. The former is managed
by Cornell University Facilities department, the latter by a
group called Cornell Plantations. Our plan was to pull the
Plantations landscape further into and in fact, completely
across the campus, linking to the gorge on the far side by
following the path of a partially buried stream. Similarly, at
Pyramid Hill, introducing a native plant landscape along the
creek system contrasts with the existing pastoral lawn and tree
landscape of the park. Different management regimes as well
as cultural biases often make these shifts difficult. In both
cases the regeneration of the forest, as well as the extension of
the ecological diversity of the plant and animal species make a
case for integration. Greater plant density in already forested
areas also helps to further reduce storm water discharge
into the creeks by slowing its flow and thus improving water
quality as it percolates through the permeable forest floor.

At St. Patrick's Island in Calgary, we wanted to restore
the forest understory. But here, the forest is unusual in that
it is composed of only one key species—the poplar. What
distinguishes the forests of this island is their detectable

age, since this species can only regenerate after a flood.
So the mature forest developed after one major flood
event, and the younger forest areas followed a more recent
one, separated by several decades. Looking closer, other
differences emerge particularly due to solar orientation: a
north-facing forest edge is more abrupt, a south-facing edge
more gradual as species persistently reach towards the
sun. This corresponds suitably with our use of the south-
facing edge for people and activities, and the north-facing
edges for animal habitat. On Dubai Nature Island, we had
to make our forest from scratch, but, similarly, only one
species was historically dominate - the mangrove (though
now virtually nonexistent there). So we designed interior
mangrove swamps, with upland areas of scattered and
diverse trees, grouped according to their irrigation needs.

Greater attention to the design of urban forests,
as agents of public health, as ecological engines,
and as cultural artifacts, is essential to structuring
confluence between human settlement and the natural
processes that precede and continue to shape it.

The Urban Forest

Urban trees offer a beautiful, cost-effective means to purify air, provide shade, reduce electricity demand and smog, and increase real estate values. We're going to need these ecosystem services, because by 2030, U.S. urban populations will rise 40% above current levels, with 1 million new residents in New York City alone, and the effects of climate change will be challenging. As just one example of climate change's urban impact, since the 1940s, summer temperatures in New York City have risen more than 7°F over surrounding suburbs due to the heat island effect.

Healthy urban canopies correlate with human health, and have been associated with lower rates of obesity, asthma and respiratory problems, increased birth weight, reduced anxiety and depression, and decreased crime and vandalism. Studies suggest that individuals who plant trees deepen their sense of place and are more likely to participate in other forms of civic activity, such as voting. Trees improve soil quality and provide biological corridors and habitat for increased biodiversity; red-tailed hawks that nest in Greenwood Cemetery and hunt in Prospect Park have limited perches between these two important landscapes, so efforts are being made to plant trees that could strengthen the corridor they need to survive.

Urban forests hold astonishing value as well (even though markets to access that value remain to be developed). For example, a 2007 analysis by the U.S. Department of Agriculture and U.S. Forest Service of all 5.2 million New York City trees revealed tree canopy covered 20.9% of the city's area; the approximately 1.35 million tons of carbon stored in their root zones was valued at about $24.9 million. Annually, New York City trees remove 42,300 tons of carbon and 2,202 tons of air pollution at a value of about $11.4 million per year. Urban trees also reduce gray infrastructure costs by storing and filtering storm water runoff and providing storm-surge protection. By some estimates, the infrastructural value of all New York City trees may be as much as $5.2 billion. It's worth noting that since completion of the 2007 survey, New York City launched MillionTreesNYC, a partnership between the New York City Department of Parks & Recreation and the New York Restoration Project (NYRP) to plant one million more trees to all five boroughs of New York by 2015.

Municipalities, including New York City, are slowly coming to understand the immense scope of services provided by urban trees. The next great urban forest challenge will be how to care for them. Perhaps in the future, well-developed markets for sequestered carbon or other ecosystem services provided by trees will fund their stewardship. Until that time, to enjoy the many benefits urban trees confer we must find a way to provide regular maintenance, just as we would to maintain any form of critical infrastructure.

Deborah Marton
Senior Vice President of Programs
New York Restoration Project

HEMLOCK BASSWOOD
M   CEDAR
BIRCH
ASH
MAPLE
PINE
OAK - CHINCAPI

FINGER LAKES — ITHACA

1 Finger Lakes Region in New York State

2 Cornell University and Ithaca New York

CORNELL MVR

The College of Human Ecology at Cornell University in Ithaca, NY, desired a "campus" for their college—a place for gathering and greater identity within the University setting. The College lies at a critical juncture within the campus landscape, where the formality and flat topography of the traditional campus quadrangles meets the steep slopes and rugged gorges that are iconic of Cornell and its surrounding geology. We sought to leverage the unique friction of these edges to strengthen the College's physical identity and establish stronger linkages to the larger campus and landscape.

College Campus Links University Landscape Systems

The new landscape at the College of Human Ecology acts catalytically on the whole of the University landscape by taking a step forward in integrating the formal landscape with the particular "wildness" of Ithaca's terrain. For this project, we increased the porosity of the borders between the campus and the gorge by extending the native plant life into the College and then on into the University. It now connects with other remnants of native plantings and creates a unified ecological and pedestrian system, improving pedestrian flows to and through the College. We also redesigned service roadways to privilege the pedestrian over vehicular movement.

A Campus of Edges for the College

With its particular location and topography, each edge of the College posed a unique situation of access and identity. Increasing the number of gathering places anchored and activated the many new pathways. Each gathering place draws on the colliding elements of the existing landscape: the quad meeting the forest, the forest meeting the gorge. We wanted to both distinguish and knit together these various forces. A variety of overlooks accentuates the vertical contrasts in the topography. Stone slabs from the local landscape provide seating throughout, further uniting the campus with its surroundings.

To create an embracing heart of a space within the College, a new central plaza, the Commons, is nestled between the historic building and its contemporary addition, the HEB. The Commons is broad enough to accommodate events and large gatherings and also makes efficient use of land situated over the parking garage. The native landscape spills into the Commons from outside, uniting it with its context. The College of Human Ecology now has its own quad which can serve both traditional quad functions and also further the unique mission of the College.

1   View of Overlook

2   View of central gathering
space, The Commons

3   Site plan

4   Stairs from the east

a   Entry plaza and
Overlook bench

b   Overlook stone

c   Central plaza paving

Project Team

Client:
Cornell University,
College of Human Ecology

Landscape Architect:
W Architecture and
Landscape Architecture LLC

Architect:
HEB
Gruzen Samton LLP

Civil Engineer:
TJ Miller

a

b

c

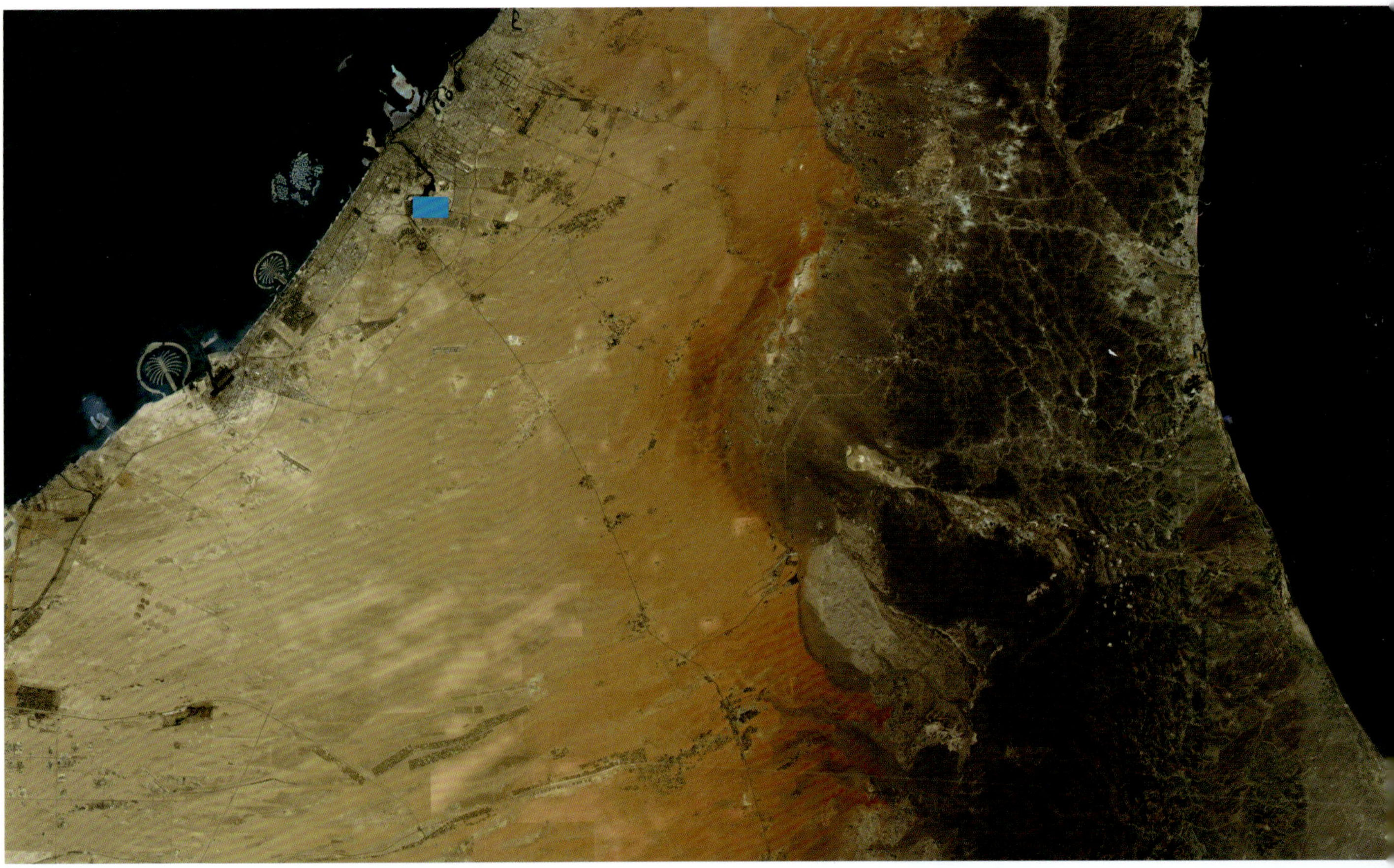

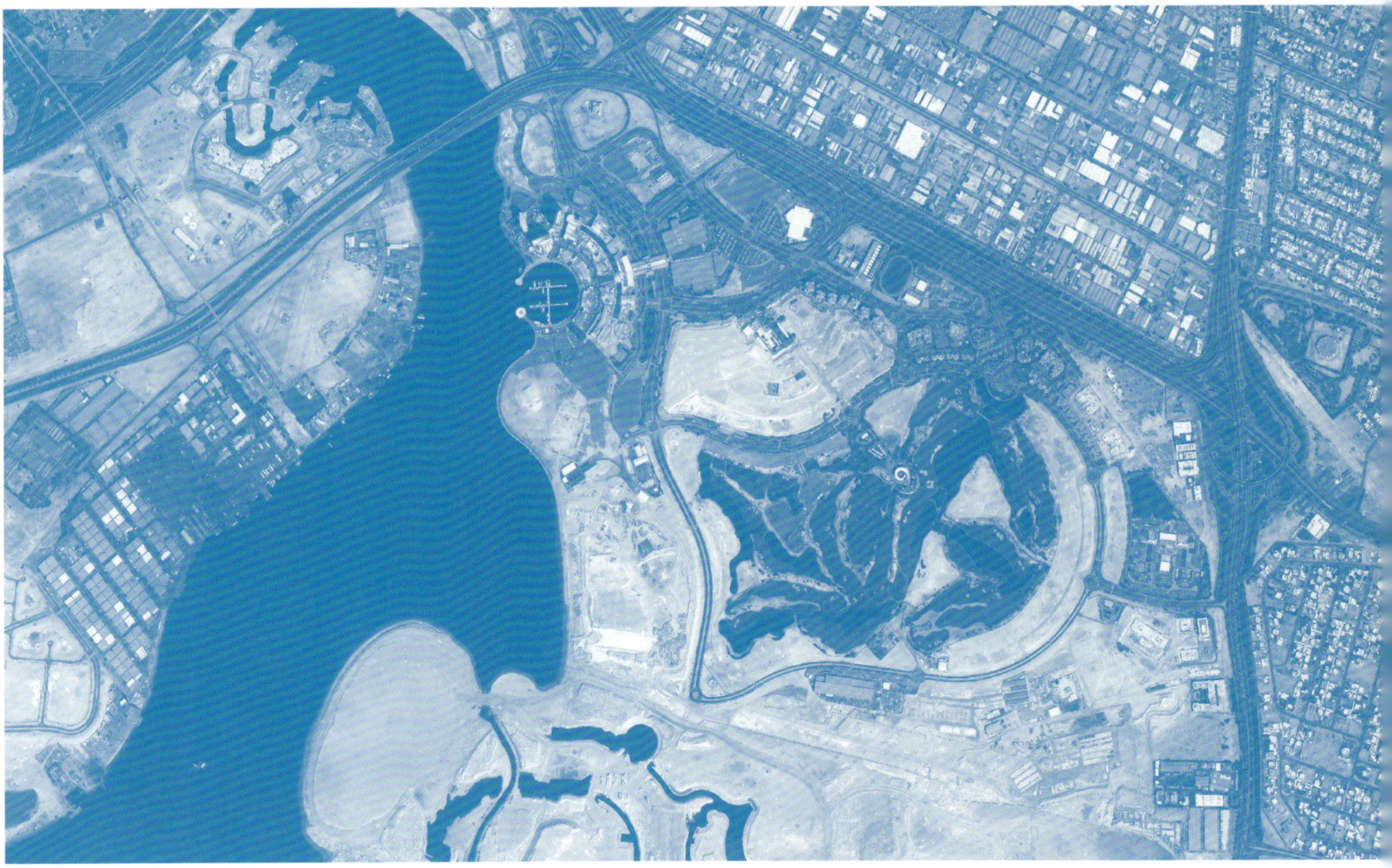

DESERT — DUBAI

With only inches of rain per year, water is a precious resource in
the UAE. Various shades of grey water reclamation irrigate much
of the open landscape. Desalination has become the main source
of sweet water, and this energy heavy process and its by products,
together with car-based development, are radically changing the
local ecology. Until last year it was the most wasteful place on
the planet, Every two years since 1998 the World Wide Fund for
Nature (WWF) has produced a global ecological footprint chart,
and the UAE has topped every chart since 2000. It is now third
place behind Qatar and Kuwait. Of course, though the UAE may
look wasteful, the United States is not far behind at number 5.

1   Peninsula of the United Arab Emirates

2   Dubai and its creek

DUBAI
NATURE ISLAND

Designing Dubai Nature Island was an exciting challenge. Dubai isn't known for its public parks or its native ecology, and this started as a competition for a bridge. Working with FXFowle Associates on the landscape for the Sheikh Rashid Bin Saeed Crossing in Dubai, we conceptualized a bridge in two segments. This created new land in the middle of the crossing, an opportunity for an island park celebrating the fragile mangrove landscape of this tidal creek. The bridge won the competition and work on the project began.

Building an island is both similar and different to adapting an existing one—patterns of interaction between the water and the land must be considered. The tidal patterns of Dubai Creek would require a park with hard outer edges to keep boating channels intact and allow for ferry access. However, we also wanted to integrate with and connect to the vanishing native ecology of the Creek. The Ras Al Khor nature preserve, with flamingos and one of the few remaining mangroves in the UAE, lies further up the Creek at its headwaters.

Our island form has a hard outer shell protecting a soft interior: the water can flow up into the middle of the island, creating a tidal salt marsh that can support native species while the hard edges can support hard infrastructure like a ferry landing, arts center, and transit hub . It is made from the dredge and excavations for the bridge foundations.

In a city often too hot for people to spend much time outside, the ubiquity of water at the park will cool the air enough to encourage pedestrian activity and outdoor recreation. The 30 new acres of mangrove will help to clean and filter the air and water around the growing city and provide precious habitat for birds and other wildlife. As urbanization continues, this area of mangroves and salt marsh will become a "central park" for the city.

1   Headwaters of the Dubai Creek with proposed bridge and Nature Island

2   View overlooking mangrove and nature center

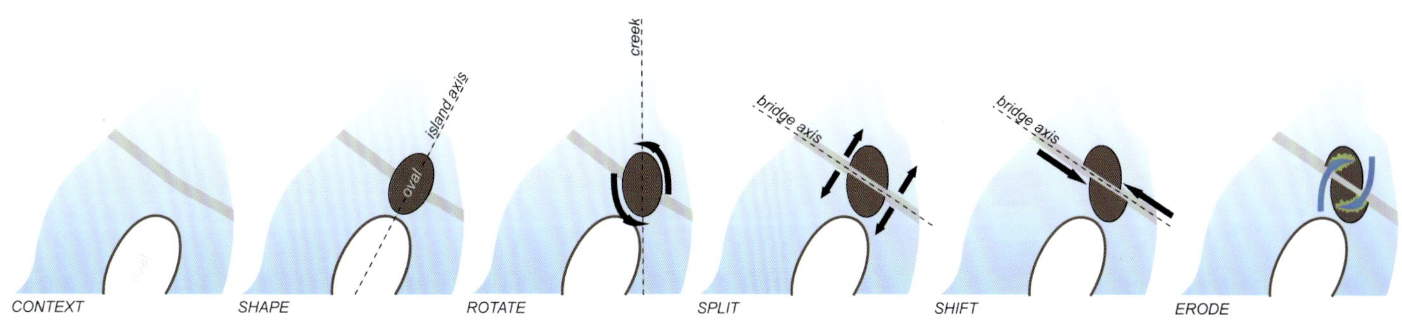

3   Diagrams showing development of island form

1997—North Pacific Gyre Garbage patch discovered by Charles Moore, a sailor returning home after Transpac race (It was predicted by NOA in 1988)

a

b

4   View of promenade edge with mangrove at the right

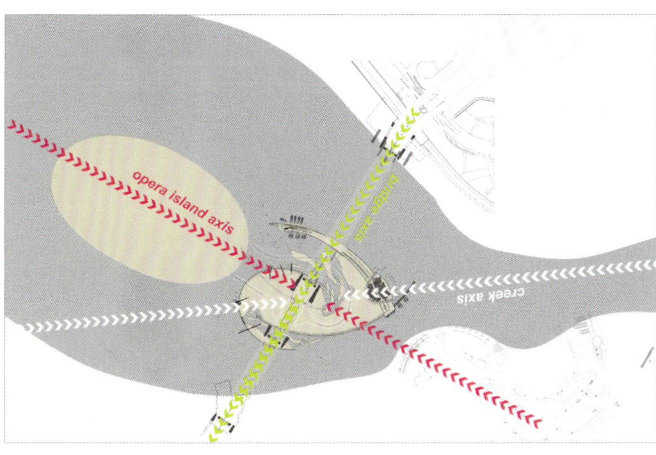

c

a   Illustrated site plan

b   Program elements

c   Various axis of island form

Project Team

Client:
Government of Dubai, Roads
and Transport Authority

Architect:
FXFowle

Structural Engineer:
Parsons Transportation

5   Plan of island and landings

CANAL DISTRICT

The overall vision for the Canal District, a planned community for 150,000 residents, is to create a vibrant "city with in a city" to live work and play. In contrast to much of the rest of Dubai, the district will be a high density, pedestrian friendly, mixed-use development. The plan promotes a compact pedestrian environment with an accessible waterfront and dynamic street life. The principles of the plan will maximize the relationship between the community and the ecology of the desert, integrating sustainable features into the landscape, infrastructure, architecture and the urban planning.

Created along a canal dug in the desert landscape near Dubai, the landscape concept takes its inspiration from the natural elements found in the indigenous desert landscape of the UAE. Al-Wadi is the Arabic name given to the carved shape the earth takes when it is eroded by a watercourse. When it rains in the desert, rainwater runs in wadis. The scale of the wadi can vary from a swale to a canyon. A trail of plants often follows it, betraying the presence of water in the soil.

The Canal District Landscape Master plan identifies 5 corridors perpendicular to the canal to carve deep into the urban fabric, linking the waterfront to a large central park. These corridors are urban parks formed like wadis to bring water and life into the built environment. While the wadis divide the development into neighborhoods, they also bring those neighborhoods together sharing their large common open spaces. The streets running along the sides of the wadis integrate buildings and landscape and include bicycle paths and walkways. Each wadi is unique and includes a source, a watercourse, a cascade, and an oasis, using recycled water from the canal. All have native vegetation commonly found in natural wadis, small springs, and pools as well as natural materials such as gravel, rocks, and boulders. These linear urban parks provide shelter and intimacy and create a microclimate that provides some relief from the harsh desert environment.

Other elements of the Landscape Master Plan include greenway systems which link the neighborhoods bike pathways and parks, and a Main Street for community gathering. A continuous linear park at the waterfront unites a variety of edge conditions and environments.

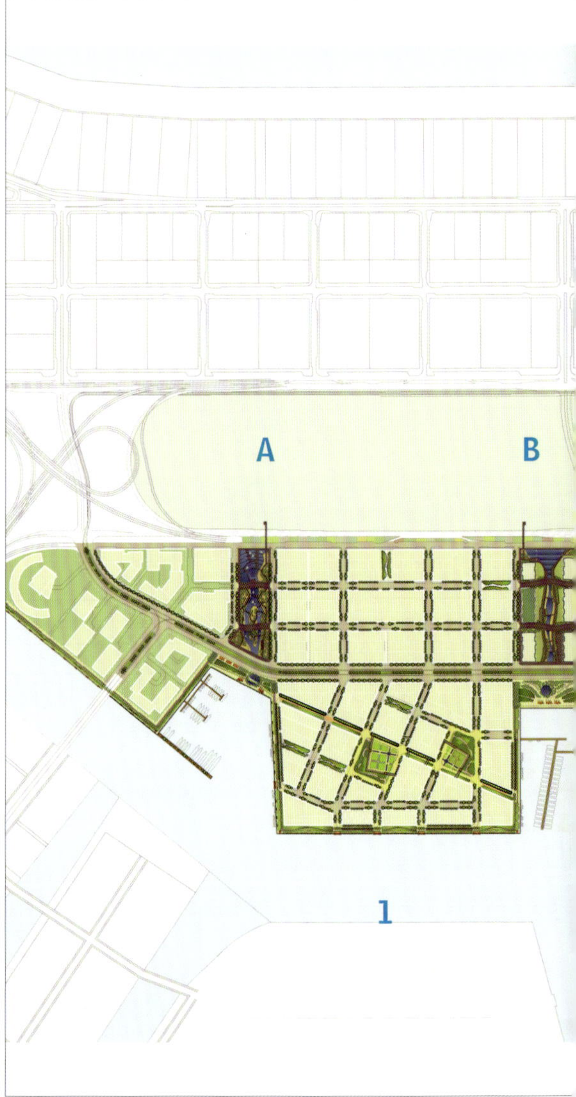

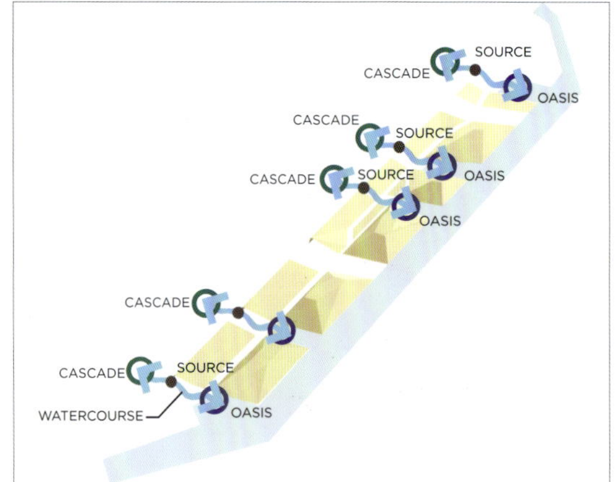

a

b

1999—W Architecture and Landscape Architecture founded
in New York City—first office at York St Dumbo

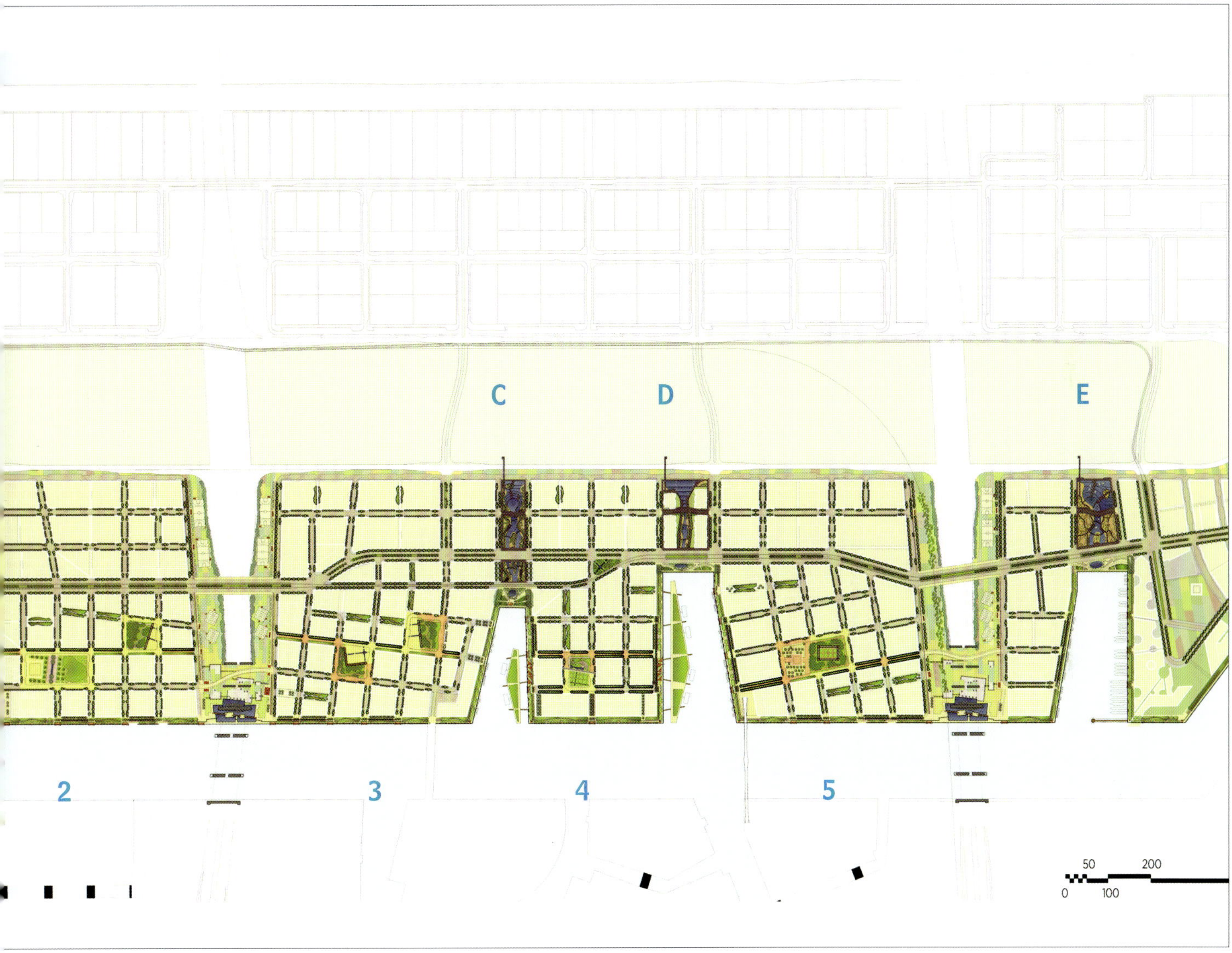

1 Illustrated Landscape Master Plan

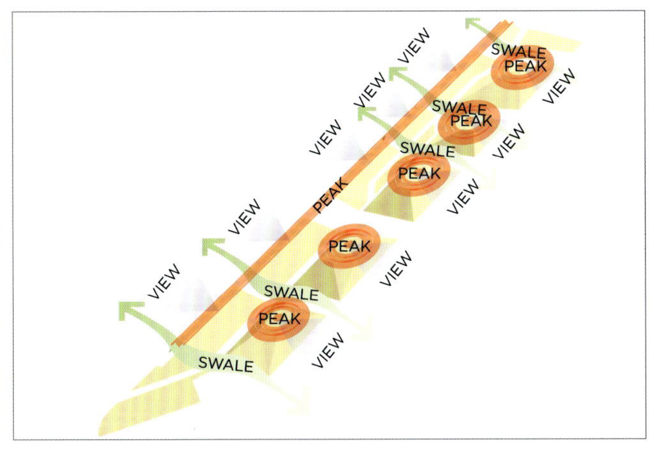

c

Project Team

Client
Dubai Waterfront, Nakheel

Architect
and Master Planner
FXFowle Architects

Landscape Master Planner
W Architecture and
Landscape Architecture

Lighting Designer
AWA Lighting Design

a Wadi parks located between neighborhoods

b Neighborhood parks located at highpoint of neighborhoods

c Topography creates views and identity

GLACIAL MORAINE — HAMILTON

"You could not step twice into the same river;
for other waters are ever flowing on to you."

Fragment 41, Heraclitus of Ephesus

1   Southwest Ohio and the
Great Miami River Valley

2   Hamilton, Ohio

OHIO HOUSE

Hamilton, Ohio is a county seat founded in 1791. At the time I was growing up, it was a prosperous town of about 85,000 people, still home to many industries. Like many former industrial cities in America, it has now shrunk to 62,000 and is struggling to find a new identity.

The town has an unusual plan worth noting: it's main street is broken in two, each end pointing at an important monument in the town center. Main Street visually terminates at the courthouse and town square, and High Street terminates in the Soldiers and Sailors Monument on the Great Miami River. Returning home for holidays, I have come to appreciate the good bones of this still proud town, but was dismayed by the growing number old buildings demolished to give way to parking lots and the many vacant storefronts of those remaining.

I purchased a vacant two storey commercial building just off the square to save one of these buildings and to create a home for myself in Hamilton. Here I could archive all my household treasures too numerous to fit in my small NYC apartment. The building was a sturdy construction in concrete and steel, with masonry bearing fire walls at either end, and an elegant limestone façade sourced from neighboring Indiana.

My renovation is an exercise in low maintenance frugality. The plan is simple and open— the exterior walls of my second floor space visible and unencumbered, encircling a new core with mechanical and plumbing requirements adjacent to the existing entrance stair rising up from the street. The existing concrete floor is exposed, polished and sealed, the existing painted wood doors reused in the core, and a sculpture by my friend Margo Sawyer acts as a railing to the newly opened stair, allowing views thru the apartment and accentuating its wonderful quality of light. Much to my surprise, I enjoy being there.

The next phase will be to find a use for the ground floor level, something that will provide activity on the street and contribute to life in town. Through research I have found that half of the ground floor was "The Eatmore" a wonderful old diner with murals on the walls where I used to have donuts with my grandfather on Saturdays, when we walked over from his florist shop on the square. As I continue to re-engage in the life of this town, the goal is to make a place of new experiences that contributes to appreciation of the opportunities for dwelling within this forgotten city infrastructure.

1   Loft Living area

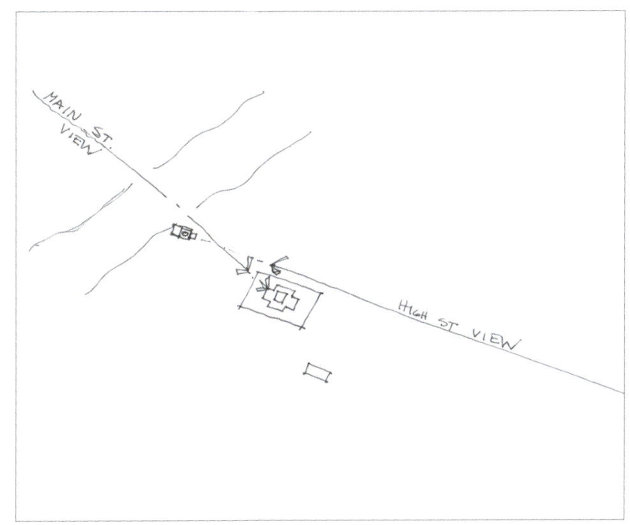

a

a   Diagram of Main St/High St axes

b   Reused doors in core

c   Reused concrete floor, sanded and sealed

d   Railing sculpture by Margo Sawyer

b

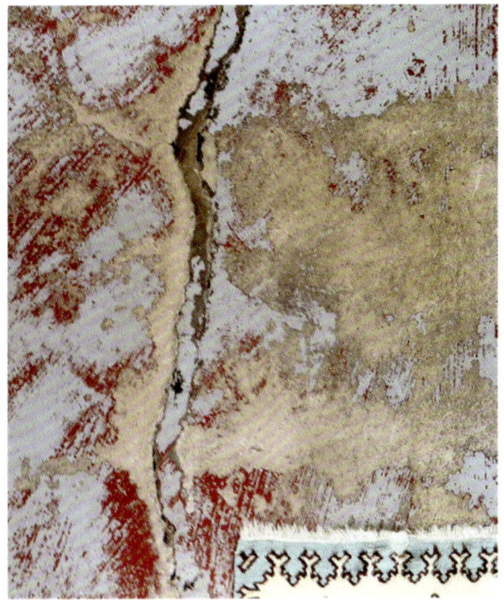

c

d

PYRAMID HILL CONFLUENCE PROJECT

Few of our projects work with the landscape in a non-urban setting. Pyramid Hill in southwestern Ohio, overlooking the Great Miami River, is a sculpture park featuring over 60 monumental works set in 265 acres of rolling hills on the outskirts of Hamilton, Ohio. Despite its rural setting, we found that the landscape in this park was actually quite disturbed. As a former farm, many areas of trees had been cleared, pines had been planted by the Conservation core in the 1930's, and the park had already cleared much of the underbrush from the wooded areas. A pastoral landscape of trees and lawn presently dominated.

In our design process, a key feature is learning about and working with the structure of the place. Our analysis pointed us to the critical importance of the creeks—the active shapers of the land. The underutilized valleys which held parking lots and restrooms were invisible assets at the heart of the park and offered an opportunity to introduce a tightly constructed series of pedestrian pathways focused on the water system.

Leaving the large pastoral landscapes of the hilltops where the sculptures are placed untouched, the Confluence Project creates a series of looped walking trails to allow visitors to focus on the detail and texture of a renewed native landscape. These loops circle three creeks cut into the glacial till of the site. Each of these is home to a different ecology. A clearing adjacent to an old stone house was an opportunity for a sunny meadow landscape with creekside wet and upland dry areas and a deck overlook. A maple woodland with an ephemeral stream offered a walk through a dry forest with little understory. The confluence of these two creates an opportunity for a moist woodland with a dense understory of shrubs and wildflowers. The Confluence Project will transform an existing asphalt parking lot at this site into a woodland garden with access to the stream bed which is littered with fossils from the Ordovician period as well as occasional Indian relics. Thus, the ecology of the three sites is dramatized and restored to improve park diversity and to provide a variety of environments and interpretive opportunities for visitors.

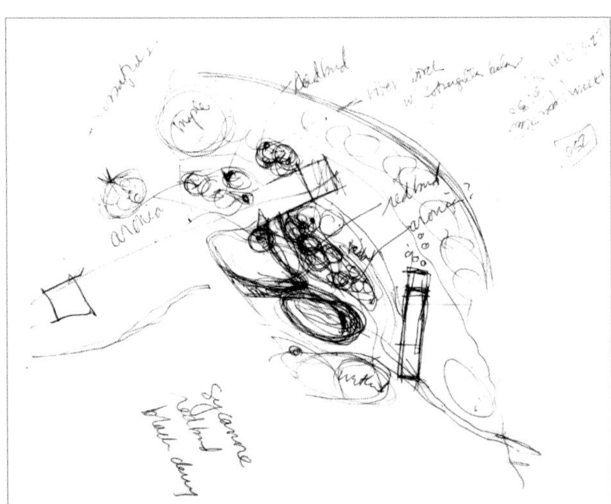

1   Sketch of plan for the pioneer native meadow

2 View from new deck to pioneer house

a

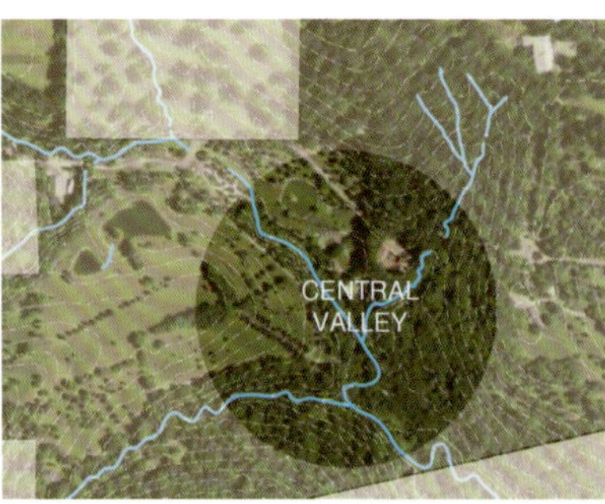

b

c

3   Existing Pyramid Hill landscape with monumental sculptures

a   Hilltop sculptures with creek in foreground

b   The confluence central valley location

c   Deck under construction

4 Meadow planting late summer

d

e

f

d Meadow planting, first year

e Meadow under construction

f Meadow under construction

W - Architecture Studio by year of entry

1999
Andrea Rhinehart Steele
Francisco Pardo

2000
Scott Murray
Andrew Vrana
Clara Sola-Morales
Amy Vona
Laquita Birch

2001
Georgina Bracone
Michel Hsiung
Scott Rae

2002
James Coleman
Vivian Mandala
Dragana Zoric
Johannes Feder
Betty Chen

2003
Sera Baldwin
Pegy Brimhall
Mayuko Ouchi
Timothy Dumbleton
Stephanie Tuerk
Lisa Switkin
Caroline Brown
Ken Mito
Iris Hooper
Saul Hayutin
Ricardo Romo-Leroux
Judith Wong
Yun Hsueh

2004
Tatiana Choulika
Kelly Flemming
Melissa Yip
Paul De Silva
Marco Brosso
Kristin Carlson
David Cunningham
Ken Mito
Amy Cooney
Glenn Garrison
Frannie Peterson

2005
Julia Murphy
James Sawyer
Grace Chen
Jeffrey Massey
Amanda Sanders
Melissa Dittmer
Boris Kolaric

2006
Michael Lavery
Runit Chhaya
Shin-lin Len
Carolyn Calder
Jennifer Rathjen

2007
Nick Koster
Martin Barry
Lauren Vasey
Benjamin Lehrer
Kate Belski

2008
2009
2010
Melany Wimpee
Amy Grigg
Hendy Bloch

2011
2012
Alison Hirsch
Danny Turgeon
Xiaowen Wu

2013
Julia Howe
Steven Yavanian
Erika Mathhias
David Mosey
Kate Cella
Darian Lu
Frannie Peterson

Acknowledgements

I would very much like to thank Michael Sorkin and Eric Sanderson for their inspiration, friendship, and generous contributions to this book. Also many friends made helpful comments and suggestions during the editing process, keeping my spirits up during the grueling process of writing, including Ray Gastil, Mark Johnson, Martin Barry, Isabelle Moutaud, and especially my daughter Lucy Struever. Alison Hirsch generously agreed to edit the four brown paper articles in a last minute crush.

The graphics were inspired by my other daughter, Sara Struever's original design for our logo and identity. Using Bell Centennial font, which she selected for us because of its functional relationship to scale issues, she devised a dynamic identity system which "wraps" the page. Caju Collective and particularly Gustavo Prado, took these same design ideas and creatively transformed them into something similar yet different for this book design.

Lastly, but most importantly, thanks to our clients who made this all possible.

Firm History

W Architecture and Landscape Architecture was founded by Barbara Wilks in the fall of 1999. After 25 years of practice in Baltimore, where she transformed waterfronts, brown-fields, campuses, infrastructures, and historic buildings and neighborhoods, Barbara moved to New York City to create a new interdisciplinary firm that focuses on urban issues. As an architect and a landscape architect, Barbara wanted her new firm to realign nature and the city.

Barbara has a Bachelor of Architecture from Cornell University and a Masters of Landscape Architecture from the University of Pennsylvania. She is honored to be a Fellow of both the American Institute of Architects and the American Society of Landscape Architects in recognition of her excellence in design. Enrique Norten joined Barbara in NYC as a partner from 2000-2001. Alex Washburn was an active partner from 2002-2006. Martin Barry has been an associate of the firm since 2012.

127 W 25th St studio

35 York St studio in Dumbo

Photography credits

Tide Point

Image 1,7
Barbara Wilks

Images 2,3, 4
Erik Kvalsvik

Image 5
Janet Rettaliata

Image 6,8
Erik Kvalsvik

**Image a 14-
15   Barbara Wilks**

**Images b,c (Pages 14-
15)   Erik Kvalsvik**

Reuse and history
Barbara Wilks, Alison
Cartwright

**Baltimore Museum
of Industry**

Image 1,2
Barbara Wilks

Clipper Mill

Image 1,2,b
Patrick Ross

Image a
Barbara Wilks

DoMa Barn

Image 1
Alan Karchmer

Image 2
Erik Kvalsvik

Image 3.4,5,6
Alan Karchmer

Image a
Alan Karchmer

Image b,c
Erik Kvalsvik

West Harlem Piers Park

Image 1,2
Alison Cartwright

Image 3
Barbara Wilks

Image 4,5,6
Alison Cartwright

Image a
Johannes Feder

Image b
Alison Cartwright

Image d
Barbara Wilks

The Edge

Image 1,2,3,4
Alison Cartwright

St Patrick's Island

Image 1,6,7,8
Barbara Wilks

Image a
Barbara Wilks

Cornell MVR

Image 1
ESTO

Image 2
Jon Reis

Image 4
ESTO

Image a
Jon Reis

Image b
ESTO

Image c
Martin Barry

Ohio House

All images
Barbara Wilks

Pyramid Hill

All images
Barbara Wilks

Published by
ORO editions
Publishers of Architecture, Art, and Design

Gordon Goff: Publisher

www.oroeditions.com
info@oroeditions.com

Copyright © 2014 by ORO editions
ISBN: 978-1-941806-12-8
10 09 08 07 06 5 4 3 2 1 First edition

Graphic Design: Caju Collective - Gustavo Prado.
Assistants: Cindy Rodriguez and Joana Batista.
Color Separations and Printing: ORO Group Ltd.
Production manager: Usana Shadday
Printed in China.

This book was printed and bound using a variety of sustainable
manufacturing processes and materials including soy-
based inks, acqueous-based varnish, VOC- and formaldehyde-
free glues, and phthalate-free laminations. The text is printed
using offset sheetfed lithographic printing process in 5 color
on 157gsm premium matt art paper with an off-line gloss
acqueous spot varnish applied to all photographs.

ORO editions makes a continuous effort to minimize the overall
carbon footprint of its publications. As part of this goal, ORO editions,
in association with Global ReLeaf, arranges to plant trees to replace
those used in the manufacturing of the paper produced for its books.
Global ReLeaf is an international campaign run by American Forests,
one of the world's oldest nonprofit conservation organizations. Global
ReLeaf is American Forests' education and action program that
helps individuals, organizations, agencies, and corporations improve
the local and global environment by planting and caring for trees.

Library of Congress data: Available upon request

For information on our distribution, please visit our website
www.oroeditions.com